STUDIES IN FILM GENRES
edited by
ANTHONY SLIDE

1. *Romantic vs. Screwball Comedy: Charting the Difference*, by Wes D. Gehring. 2003
2. *Screening Politics: The Politician in American Movies, 1931–2001*, by Harry Keyishian. 2003
3. *People Like Ourselves: Portrayals of Mental Illness in the Movies*, by Jacqueline Noll Zimmerman. 2003

People Like Ourselves

*Portrayals of Mental Illness
in the Movies*

Jacqueline Noll Zimmerman

Studies in Film Genres, No. 3

The Scarecrow Press, Inc.
Lanham, Maryland, and Oxford
2003

SCARECROW PRESS, INC.

Published in the United States of America
by Scarecrow Press, Inc.
A wholly owned subsidiary of The Rowman & Littlefield Publishing Group, Inc.
4501 Forbes Boulevard, Suite 200, Lanham, Maryland 20706
www.scarecrowpress.com

PO Box 317
Oxford
OX2 9RU, UK

British Library Cataloguing in Publication Information Available

Library of Congress Cataloging-in-Publication Data

Zimmerman, Jacqueline Noll, 1948–
  People like ourselves : portrayals of mental illness in the movies / Jacqueline Noll
Zimmerman.
        p. cm. — (Studies in film genres ; no. 3)
        Includes bibliographical references and index.
    ISBN 0-8108-4876-7 (cloth : alk. paper)
    1. Mental illness in motion pictures. I. Title. II. Series.
PN1995.9.M463Z56 2003
791.43'653—dc21

                                                                    2003010896

♾ᵀᴹ The paper used in this publication meets the minimum requirements of
American National Standard for Information Sciences—Permanence of
Paper for Printed Library Materials, ANSI/NISO Z39.48-1992.
Manufactured in the United States of America.

For my family

~

Contents

Acknowledgments   xi

Introduction   xiii

Chapter 1   The Price of Conformity: The False Self   1
             The Madness of King George
             Now, Voyager
             Fear Strikes Out
             To Kill a Mockingbird
             Dead Poets Society
             A Woman under the Influence
             One Flew over the Cuckoo's Nest
             Nuts
             Frances
             An Angel at My Table

Chapter 2   The Denial of Reality   21
             The Snake Pit
             The Three Faces of Eve
             Raintree County
             Suddenly, Last Summer
             The Caretakers

Splendor in the Grass
David and Lisa
Ordinary People
As Good as It Gets

Chapter 3   Hitchcock, Chaos, and the Devils
        of Unreason   47
Rebecca
Spellbound
Marnie
Vertigo
Shadow of a Doubt
The Man Who Knew Too Much
The Wrong Man
Psycho
The Birds

Chapter 4   Women Who Can't Forget   67
Sunset Boulevard
A Streetcar Named Desire
Don't Bother to Knock
The Rain People
Summer Wishes, Winter Dreams
Plenty
Losing Chase
Possessed
Play Misty for Me
Fatal Attraction
Sophie's Choice
Beloved

Chapter 5   Divine Madness: Poets, Prophets,
        and Demons   91
A Beautiful Mind
A Fine Madness
Finding Forrester
Benny & Joon
Shine

Agnes of God
Equus
The Fisher King
Lilith
Sophie's Choice
Cross Creek

Chapter 6   War: A Battle for the Mind and Spirit   113
             The Best Years of Our Lives
             The Caine Mutiny
             Captain Newman, M.D.
             The Man in the Gray Flannel Suit
             Coming Home
             Born on the Fourth of July
             Chattahoochee
             Saving Private Ryan
             Platoon
             The Thin Red Line
             The Deer Hunter
             Full Metal Jacket
             Apocalypse Now
             King of Hearts

Chapter 7   Violence and Mental Illness:
               A Good Movie Is Hard to Find   131
             Shock Corridor
             Psycho
             The Shining
             The Silence of the Lambs
             Plenty
             Nuts
             Repulsion
             Girl, Interrupted
             Taxi Driver
             Raging Bull
             Affliction

Notes   145

Sources Cited	147
Films Discussed and/or Cited	151
Index	157
About the Author	166

~

Acknowledgments

I wish to express my gratitude to the many friends and colleagues who showed an interest in this project.

In particular, I want to thank Richard Hudgens, M.D., professor of psychiatry at the Washington University School of Medicine, who encouraged me to write about this topic, shared his insights, and reviewed a draft of the manuscript.

Most of all, I thank my husband, Roger Val Zimmerman, retired professor of humanities and liberal arts, Lewis and Clark Community College, for his tireless contributions to this book. His experience as a poet, an editor, and a teacher of writing and literature was invaluable to me. This book would not have happened without his support.

INTRODUCTION

~

Madness and the
Human Condition

In Shakespeare's great tragedy, Prince Hamlet pretends to be mad to learn the truth of his father's, the king's, death. Hamlet knows that in the sixteenth century, as in centuries past, people will disregard the words and actions of a madman. Nor will they consider him capable of plotting and executing revenge. Hamlet's pretense is the perfect cover for his intentions. By feigning madness, he becomes, in a sense, invisible to those in the court whom he distrusts. Disarmed by his insanity, they reveal their wrongdoing and guilt. Polonius, the lord chamberlain, suspects as much when he says of Hamlet's behavior, "Though this be madness . . . there is method in't" (II, ii, 203–204).

Shakespeare's use of the madman, or the fool, in *Hamlet*, *King Lear*, and other plays appealed wildly to the vast numbers of illiterate and uneducated who attended the theater. Hamlet's disheveled looks, rude manners, and bawdy puns enjoyed a raucous response from the pit. One might say that Shakespeare exploited the figure of the deranged mind for its theatricality. In plot, character, and theme, however, *Hamlet* revolves on this central image and theme of madness. The outward signs of madness can be easily mimicked, but the complexity of Hamlet's condition cannot be so easily articulated. The prince scolds his onetime friends Rosencrantz and Guildenstern for thinking that they can "pluck out" the "heart" of his "mystery" (III, ii, 351–352)—easily identify the cause and nature of his condition, be it derangement or something else. The appearance of madness makes visible Hamlet's inner turmoil, but it cannot identify or explain it.

Madness is part of the human condition, not separate from it. Shakespeare's use of madness in *Hamlet* is effective because the character is more than the outward appearance of madness, more than what is so often a stereotype. Ultimately, Shakespeare's play is concerned with the human condition and with the shared plight of humans who can feel small and powerless. Always, Shakespeare brings the audience back to the humanity of the character, whether sane or insane, and his commonality with all other humans.

It should be no surprise that madness has also been a popular subject of American movies. In film as on the stage, madness can be exquisitely visible. Consequently, the mentally disturbed person has been a frequent object of exploitation in the movies. In appearance, gesture, and speech, the insane person has been portrayed as an outsider and, at the worst, an alien who fascinates and horrifies the audience. Some critics even say that the majority of American movies that depict mental illness exploit it. Otto F. Wahl in *Media Madness: Public Images of Mental Illness* acknowledges that "films about mental illness . . . have included many well-crafted and critically acclaimed . . . ventures" (4), but he concludes that "media images of mental illness do not measure up well" (12–13). Mental health advocate Rosalynn Carter makes the following assessment in her 1998 *Helping Someone with Mental Illness*: "Of the hundreds of movies in which psychiatrists or psychiatric hospitals have been depicted, we need only think of *One Flew over the Cuckoo's Nest* to understand how negatively they can be characterized" (230).

Although the hospital and the staff are portrayed negatively in Milos Forman's 1975 film, those portrayals do not support Carter's larger claim that the movie depicts mental illness and psychiatry inaccurately and insensitively. In fact, since the 1940s, when the first notable American movies about mental illness were produced, numerous films, including *One Flew over the Cuckoo's Nest*, have created honest, memorable images of the internal chaos experienced with schizophrenia, paranoia, depression, and a variety of other conditions. Even some early films, such as *The Snake Pit* (1948), *Don't Bother to*

Knock (1952), and *Fear Strikes Out* (1957), present their central characters sympathetically, albeit trapped in stereotypes or victimized by doctors, nurses, and institutions ill equipped to help them.

The best movies have also explored the complexity of mental illness, the "mystery" of it, to use Hamlet's word. Like *Hamlet*, some movies have succeeded in getting beyond the outward appearance and portraying the underlying humanity of the character who is severely mentally ill. Ron Howard's *A Beautiful Mind* manages just that by representing the voices a person with schizophrenia hears as imaginary characters on screen. A number of films have explored the very nature of madness, examining, as Sidney Lumet's *Equus* does, the relationship of madness to passion or, as Norman Jewison's *Agnes of God* does, its kinship to ecstasy or rapture. Other films, such as John Cassavetes's *A Woman under the Influence*, consider the difficulty of defining madness and understanding its relationship to perception. These and other movies not only reject the stereotypes associated with mental illness.[1] They also question the labels, approaches, and treatments applied by the established medical community.

People who suffer from schizophrenia, paranoia, and other serious mental illnesses often exhibit an otherness. They do not fit the norm, either in their speech patterns, their facial expressions, the way they dress, or a combination of features and aspects. Forman's film captures this differentness in R. P. McMurphy and the other patients on the ward masterfully, without exploiting it. Instead, *One Flew over the Cuckoo's Nest* seeks to uncover the relationship of the otherness to sanity, or the norm, and thereby to contribute to an understanding not only of madness but of the human condition. In its depiction of the iron-willed Nurse Ratched and the mannequin-like hospital attendants, for example, *One Flew over the Cuckoo's Nest* showcases both the general population's fear of mental patients as aliens and the need to control or overpower them, sometimes disguised, whether knowingly or unknowingly, as caregiving.

In this book I am concerned not with the hundreds of movies that exploit certain myths and stereotypes of the mentally ill, although I will identify and discuss some of those false notions. I will not discuss the movies that exploit the subject for horror or violence. I am concerned instead with American films that treat the subject honestly, increase the audience's understanding of the subject, and challenge viewers' assumptions and attitudes. Whether they are dramas, thrillers, or comedies, American movies that portray mental illness intelligently tell moviegoers not only about the way the person suffering with schizophrenia or paranoia, even simple neurosis, sees reality and relates to it, but also about the way the so-called normal person perceives and interprets the mentally ill person and defines reality.

Mental illness is, first, exactly that—illness—and the discussions in *People Like Ourselves: Portrayals of Mental Illness in the Movies* take into account current medical knowledge and treatment of severe mental illnesses, such as schizophrenia and depression. The diagnoses and causes of mental illness, it must be recognized, are myriad and complex. Mental illness can have social and psychological elements, such as upbringing and traumatic events, as sources or as contributing factors. Many major illnesses, such as schizophrenia, are now known to be linked to physiological factors. In any patient, etiology might involve all of these categories of causes. Diagnosis is similarly complex. The symptoms of one person who is diagnosed as having bipolar disease are not identical to those of another person who has this illness. The concern of *People Like Ourselves* is not with diagnosis and etiology—those are the concerns of psychiatrists and research scientists.

Mental illness is, in addition to illness, a part of the human condition. According to the U. S. Surgeon General's 1999 report on mental health, severe mental disorders afflict about one in five Americans (report overview). Increasingly, even Americans who do not experience severe illness seek counseling and medication for stress, anxiety, and other emotional problems. The concern of *People Like Ourselves*, therefore, is with commonality. This book explores the themes that unite the mentally ill with people everywhere. These common themes dramatically demonstrate that people who suffer from serious mental illness, like people with heart disease and cancer, are people like ourselves.

Madness, insanity, mental illness—whatever the general term used—it remains a mystery in many aspects. Although much progress has been made in recent decades in understanding mental illness and improving treatments, much remains to be known. As in *Hamlet*, mental illness often manifests visually dramatic signs. Prince Hamlet chides his friends for thinking that by these signs they can understand his derangement. They might better understand his illness by first know-ing his human predicament. As a number of the best movies demon-strate, a recognition of the shared human experience that underlies mental illness can illuminate this too often misunderstood condition.

~

CHAPTER ONE

The Price of Conformity
The False Self

In *The Madness of King George*, when George (Nigel Hawthorne) is recovering from a bout of madness, the chancellor remarks that the king seems more himself. George responds, "I've always been myself, even when I was ill. Only now I seem myself and that's the important thing. I have remembered how to seem." The king expresses the human tendency to be various selves, most notably a public self and a private self. The Scottish psychoanalyst-philosopher R. D. Laing points out in *The Divided Self* that most people tend to present in public a self that is not completely true.[2] It is a need for survival that prompts such deception. The rising young manager who seems eager to take on risks and challenges may secretly harbor an intense fear of failure, but he fully knows how he must *seem* in the workplace.

In the 1994 film directed by Nicholas Hytner, a sign of King George's recovery is that he knows the difference between the two selves, who he is and who he must seem to be. As Laing wrote, however, seeming to be someone in order to fit social expectations or requirements can result in a divided self, in which a person is alienated from a sense of who he actually is. The "false self," as Laing termed it, that the person dons to function in society estranges the person from his "true self" (104–105).

In portraying madness and mental illness, the movies frequently dramatize the conflict of a divided self. Many films show people struggling against the all-too-common pressure to conform. From *Now, Voyager* of 1942 to *The Madness of King George* and other films of the 1990s, characters fight to discover themselves and be themselves, while living in a world whose conventions they violate or abhor. In the process some of these movies show the power of the forces of conformity: the domineering parent, the authority figures of social institutions, and the generally accepted social conventions and mores of everyday living.

More than fifty years since its production, *Now, Voyager*, directed by Irving Rapper, continues to capture the timelessness of this conflict of self and society. The central character, Charlotte Vale (Bette Davis), is the only daughter in a straight-laced, upper-crust Bostonian family, and the story is her struggle toward self-discovery. Unmarried, dowdy, and painfully reserved, Charlotte is the spinster aunt of the family. This public self is the product of Charlotte's compliance with her tyrannical mother's expectations of a dutiful daughter. The widowed Mrs. Vale (Gladys Cooper) demands of Charlotte an unfaltering adherence to old-fashioned rules of propriety and the submissive obedience of a companion and servant. Mrs. Vale controls nearly every aspect of her daughter's behavior and life—her wardrobe, her hairstyle, even her diet.

Charlotte has a private self, too. Behind the locked door of her upper-story bedroom, she secretly smokes cigarettes, reads novels not on her mother's prescribed reading list, and expresses her creativity by carving ornamental boxes from ivory. The public Charlotte and the private Charlotte, however, are at war, and the character is on the verge of a nervous breakdown. In the opening sequence, Charlotte's caring sister-in-law Lisa (Ilka Chase) has brought a renowned psychiatrist to the Vale house to visit with Charlotte and, unbeknownst to her, assess her mental state. In spite of her shyness and alienation from the world, the doctor (Claude Rains) manages to establish a rapport with her and learn something of the price she has paid in conforming to her mother's desires. At the end of the sequence, he speaks reprovingly to Mrs. Vale of her daughter's right as a person to discover herself, "to discover her own mistakes" and grow in self-knowledge.

Charlotte spends the next three months at Cascade, the psychiatrist's Vermont sanatorium. There, she is brought back from depression and near mental collapse. When she leaves the hospital, however, her journey is only beginning, for she must now learn more about herself, her likes and dislikes, her tastes, values, and needs. Just before she leaves, her doctor gives her a piece of paper containing some words from Walt Whitman, the American poet and the great celebrator of the self and the individual. She recites them: "Untold want by life and land near granted, / Now, voyager, sail thou forth to seek and find."

The rest of the movie chronicles Charlotte's voyage through romance and loss to self-knowledge and a healthy acceptance of herself and others. She is transformed from an "ugly duckling," her mother's description of Charlotte when she is out of earshot, to a vibrant, independent woman of the forties. In important ways she violates the conventions and respectability her mother espoused. On an ocean cruise following her stay at Cascade, Charlotte falls in love with a married man, Jerry Durrance (Paul Henreid). Although they do not marry, because of his obligations to his children and an ailing wife, she rejects a proposal from a wealthy Boston widower whose name would bring added prestige to the Vale family. Although she remains single, she fulfills a need to contribute to a family, as the surrogate mother to Jerry's twelve-year-old daughter, in whom Charlotte sees a mirror image of herself as a child forced to submit to the cruel will of an unloving, tyrannical mother.

More than a decade later, in 1957, *Fear Strikes Out* portrayed another protagonist who becomes mentally sick, partially due to a divided self. Directed by Robert Mulligan and produced by Alan Pakula, this film biography of baseball player Jimmy Piersall (Anthony Perkins) focuses on the character's battle with mental illness in his early career. There is a hint that Piersall's illness was to some degree hereditary; in the movie both Jimmy and his father (Karl Malden) allude to the fact that Jimmy's mother was away often when he was growing up. The contributing factor that is dramatized in the movie, however, is Jimmy's domineering father. From the time that Jimmy is a young boy, his father pushes him to be a great ball player. His father is relentless in this pursuit, dictating when his son practices, when he sleeps, and what he eats, and denying him the social activities of an ordinary boy and adolescent. Viewers watch the son become isolated in the world of his father's dreams.

Mulligan masterfully uses images of fences to portray the young ballplayer's growing isolation and fear of failure. One of the first images in the film is the fence that encloses the Piersalls' backyard, where Jimmy and his father practice. The fence that separates the character from the outside world also creates a cage. In an early practice scene, Jimmy's hand throbs from the pitches his dad is throwing him. He winces, however, only when he is retrieving a ball from the side of the garage, out of view of his father. As the camera focuses on Piersall, wedged in the corner of the yard, flanked by the fence and the garage, the metaphor of a caged animal is clear. The false, conforming self cannot know freedom.

In the movie's climax the fence is again the central image. Piersall is playing for the Boston Red Sox but crumbling under the stress. In a game against Chicago, he is under intense pressure to get a hit. Camera shots accent the fence that separates Jimmy from the spectators, most notably his father. After long, excruciating minutes of nearly striking out, he gets not only a hit but a homer. As he rounds home plate, he grabs hold, hysterically, of the fence. "How was that?" he asks. "Was it good enough?" He begins climbing the fence, wildly trying to escape the field. His breakdown is complete when, as team members try to subdue him, he picks up a bat and begins striking out at them to defend himself, now trapped not only by fear and a sense of isolation but by paranoia.

The character's behavior is a natural progression of the fears he has felt for a long time, and Mulligan is careful not to sensationalize the scene. The film up to this point has chronicled Piersall's perceptions. Just after he has been offered and has accepted at his father's insistence a position with Boston, playing shortstop rather than outfield, for which he has spent his life training, he panics. It's evening and he goes to Fenway Park. As he stands there, he imagines the calls of the crowd and then is paralyzed by fear. Helped by Perkins's deep-set, brooding eyes, the character's face is frozen in an image of fear.

In *Now, Voyager*, very little of Charlotte's hospitalization and treatment is shown. Mulligan gives considerable time to Piersall's subsequent hospitalization and slow recovery, but is careful not to sensationalize this portion of the story. Although the state mental hospital looks more luxurious than one might associate with the typical state institution of the 1950s, the doctor who treats Piersall and the treatment he receives are depicted realistically. Electroshock therapy is administered, but off screen and only to shock the patient from a state of withdrawal. Primarily the treatment consists of long, intense counseling sessions, and the recovery is neither sudden nor miraculous. In the concluding sequence it is clear that Jimmy Piersall will struggle for some time to continue to battle his fears.

Another Mulligan–Pakula masterpiece uses a secondary character to show the price of conformity. *To Kill a Mockingbird* (1962), based on Harper Lee's Pulitzer Prize–winning novel, has as its main plot the story of a Southern white lawyer, Atticus Finch (Gregory Peck), defending in 1930s Maycomb, Alabama, a black man, Tom Robinson (Brock Peters), who is accused of raping a white woman, Mayella Ewell. Its subplot concerns the fascination of Atticus's children, ten-year-old Jem (Philip Alford) and six-year-old Scout (Mary Badham), with their neighbor, Arthur "Boo" Radley (Robert Duvall), reputedly a ghoulish maniac who roams the neighborhood at night, scratching at screen doors and peering into windows.

The importance of this subplot to the film's theme is signaled by the opening shot. The movie opens with a close-up of a cigar box, a child's hands lifting the lid to reveal the keepsakes of childhood: two carved dolls, a watch, and a pocketknife, among the treasures. As viewers learn during the film, those treasures are gifts that have been given to the children by their neighbor, not Boo Radley the maniac but Arthur Radley the troubled recluse.

Whether seen as a lunatic or as a recluse, this most memorable of minor American film characters is only a shadow of an earlier self. Boo the lunatic is a false self, not in the Laingian sense, but as a stereotype imposed by others on the character. As Jem describes him to their friend Dill, who visits Maycomb each summer, staying with his Aunt Rachel, Boo is six-and-a-half-feet tall, eats raw squirrels, has a long scar down his face and yellow, rotten teeth, and drools constantly. The children's imaginations are fuelled by the nasty whispers of the town gossips. Pointing to the Radley house, Miss Rachel warns Dill, "There's a maniac lives there." According to legend, Boo once stabbed his father with a pair of scissors and then returned coolly to what he was doing. His father, claiming "no Radley's going to any asylum," agreed to have him locked up for a time in the courthouse basement.

Arthur the harmless recluse is the product of a tyrannical father's up-bringing. For as long as anyone can remember, Arthur has been confined to his father's house, living in the unique prison Mr. Radley's iron will has constructed for him. "The meanest man in town," Jem tells Dill, Mr. Radley keeps Boo chained to the bed. To the people of Maycomb, Arthur is a shadow; he remains unseen behind the closed doors and shuttered windows of the Radley house.

Jem, Scout, and Dill are determined to get Boo Radley to come out or at least to lay eyes on him. Dill dares Jem to run up and touch the Radley house. Scout props herself in an old car tire, and they roll her down the street. When she crashes at the foot of the Radley porch, Jem rescues her, dizzy and shaken, runs up the steps, and slaps the front door.

Their most daring attempt occurs one summer night when they decide to sneak up to the Radley house and get a peek at Boo through a window. Like characters in the ghost stories they read, they creep to the rear of the house and through a garden, negotiating a creaking fence gate and porch steps. As Jem crawls to the porch window, the shadow of a man looms above him, hands outstretched as if to grab him. Nursery-room music gives way to more ominous tones, Dill and Scout see the shadow, and they bury their faces in their hands. The shadow recedes, and the children run home. En route Jem manages to get his pants tangled on the fence and has to abandon them there.

With little success, Atticus strongly discourages this nonsense. One night at bedtime Scout's curiosity about Boo gets the best of her, and she asks Atticus if Boo really looks in her window at night. In exasperation, Atticus tells her, " . . . leave those poor people alone. I want you to stay away from their house and stop tormenting them."

Atticus's respect for the ill Boo Radley as another human being is part of the movie's larger theme of tolerance. It is a message that Atticus works to imbue in his children. When Scout has troubles her first day at school, Atticus urges her to realize that it is also the first day for the new first-grade teacher. "If you learn a single trick, Scout," he says, "you'll get along a lot better with all kinds of folks. You never really understand a person until you consider things from his point of view, till you climb inside of his skin and walk around in it."

As the trial of Tom Robinson nears, opposition in town to Atticus grows. The ignorance and narrow-mindedness that characterize so many citizens' attitudes toward Boo Radley similarly shape their attitudes toward and relations with black people. Bob Ewell, the barely literate, drunken ne'er-do-well father of Mayella, is the racist extreme of this narrow thinking. The upright citizens of Maycomb condemn such vulgarity as his, but they are not above "high talk" that Atticus should not do much to defend Tom.

In Bob Ewell, Jem begins to see that there are greater things to fear than Boo. One evening Jem accompanies Atticus to the Robinson house to talk with Tom's wife, Helen. While there, Jem witnesses Bob Ewell's menacing hatefulness when Ewell, standing on the road, snarls at Atticus, "You nigger lover." Back home on the front porch, Jem waits while his father drives Calpurnia, their housekeeper, home. The trees sway gently. Then the Radley porch swing creaks. The stillness of the night is punctuated by the screeching of night hawks. In brief seconds the film captures Jem's terror as he bolts from the porch and runs down the street, calling "Atticus."

As Jem and Scout learn of the real evils in the world, they also come to see Boo Radley's humanity. When Jem and Scout find two carved soap dolls in the hollow of a tree at the edge of the Radley property, they know the gifts are intended for them: the dolls closely resemble them. That night Jem confides to Scout that he has found other things in the hollow, and he shows her the contents of the cigar box. He also confides that the night he returned to the Radley backyard to retrieve his pants, he found them folded and hanging over the fence, "sorta like they [Boo] was expecting me," he says.

Following that conversation, the voice-over narration by the now-grown Scout tells us, "It was to be a long time before Jem and I talked about Boo again." In fact, they do not talk again about Boo until months after Tom Robinson's trial and its tragic aftermath. It is Halloween, and Boo Radley finally comes out.

Scout is to be in a pageant at school, and Jem escorts her. She reminds us that "I still looked for Boo every time I went by the Radley place." Later, as she and Jem walk home in the dark, they hear eerie noises all too appropriate for Halloween: the wind rustling leaves, a dog barking, and then, the sound of footsteps following them.

Jem and Scout are attacked by Bob Ewell, and it is Arthur Radley who has ventured out of his house to save them. He carries the badly injured Jem home and takes refuge behind the door of Jem's bedroom. When Scout finally sees him face to face, she knows him without being told who he is: "Hey, Boo." Pale and timid, ghostlike in his appearance, Boo smiles gently at her. The childlike innocence and the warmth of that smile belie, in one moment, all the frightening images that have stigmatized Boo Radley. Atticus reinforces his message of understanding and tolerance when he extends his hand to shake Boo's hand and says, "Thank you, Arthur. Thank you for my children."

Like *To Kill a Mockingbird*, *Dead Poets Society* is a coming-of-age story. Also like *To Kill a Mockingbird*, it uses a secondary character to comment on self and sanity, but it shows the character's active struggle against the conformity imposed by his father. Directed by Peter Weir and written by Tom Schulman, this 1989 film is about a group of boys attending Welton Academy, a tough, elite New England prep school, in 1959 and experiencing the ordeals of adolescence. The guide and shaman for their rite of passage is the new English teacher, John Keating (Robin Williams), who himself attended Welton and now wants to inspire his students to get the most from life. The students respond in various ways to his teaching.

On the first day of class Keating captivates his young audience by leading them out to the hall and having them study the photographs of past students and athletes on display in the trophy case. As his students gaze at the faces in the photos, he chants, "Carpe diem." "Seize the day," he tells them, because tomorrow no one is anything more than food for the worms. Keating's message is not that of the hedonist; it is not so simplistic as "eat, drink, and be merry." "Make your lives extraordinary," he implores. As he guides them in their study of literature, he expands the message. They are to "suck . . . the marrow of life," as Henry David Thoreau, one of Keating's heroes and mentors, says in *Walden*. Rather than blindly accept or resign themselves to the opinions of others, they are to find their own perspective and form their own ideas. They are to do this not by living vicariously, but by living the life of imagination and following their dreams.

Thoreau's words are the motto of the Dead Poets Society, a club that Keating and some of his classmates formed when they were at Welton. When Neil Perry (Robert Sean Leonard) sees the Dead Poets Society mentioned in an old yearbook, he and some of the other students who seem most taken with the new teacher want to know about it. Keating describes it as something of a secret society whereby the members met occasionally at night in a nearby cave and read poetry aloud. They were a group of "Romantics," he says. He cautions Neil, however, saying he is not sure how the current administration would look upon such activities.

It is Neil who is most inspired by Keating. He rallies the others to form a new Dead Poets Society, and Keating leaves on Neil's desk the copy of *Five Centuries of Verse* with Thoreau's words inscribed on one of the front pages. The camera focuses for a moment on the flashlight that Neil takes from his room and then uses that first night they venture to the cave to guide his classmates through the darkness and fog. Once in the cave they timidly circle, these tribal initiates, round a fire that sputters and smokes and threatens to drive them back to the walls of Welton. In time, however, they make the cave theirs as they read poetry, tell stories, and dream dreams.

On that first night Neil reads from Lord Tennyson's poem "Ulysses," in which the poet writes about the will "To strive, to seek, to find, and not to yield." The traveler-ruler-hero of Greek myth speaks from the vantage of old age about the need to move forward, "to seek a newer world," even though he is weakened by time and experience. "Some work of noble note, may yet be done," Tennyson says (1892).

Neil's selection from Tennyson is both ironic and poignant, ironic because of the character's youth and poignant because of his inability throughout his short life to do anything but yield, in order to please, not to offend, others, most importantly his father. In an early scene, the day the boys arrive at the academy for the new term, Neil's father (Kurtwood Smith) stops by his son's room to tell him to drop one of his extracurricular activities. In front of his friends, Neil tries to reason with his father, explaining that he is to be assistant editor of the annual and it is too late to get someone else for the job. His father takes him into the hall and reprimands him: "Don't you ever dispute me in public." The father is adamant that Neil succeed at Welton and go on to medical school; those are his plans for his son. Neil's nervousness around this unbending, authoritarian figure is clear from the start: his voice cracks, he punctuates his responses in military fashion with "Sir," and, when his friends ask how he can let his father rule his life, Neil lies, "I don't give a damn about any of it."

In the darkness of the cave, however, Neil begins to encounter other aspects of his self, most notably his dream of being an actor. With a growing determination to seize the day, he auditions for and gets the part of Puck in Shakespeare's comedy *A Midsummer Night's Dream*, being produced at Henley Hall, the nearby girls school. As he begins to realize his dream, he also finds a new joy and confidence, expressed in humor and generosity with his friends. When his father learns of his involvement in the play, he predictably shows up at school, reviles his son for his deception and his "stupidity" in pursuing acting, and tells Neil he is through with the play. "You will not let me down," he orders.

Neil refuses to yield but seeks advice from Keating, who listens compassionately and urges Neil to talk honestly with his father about his "passion" for acting and to show his father his "conviction." Neil knows such efforts would be futile, and through his tears, he laughs, "I'm trapped," recalling an image from an earlier film, of Jimmy Piersall caged in his backyard. At this point the conclusion to Neil's dilemma is inevitable.

The son defies his father and performs magnificently as Puck on opening night. Between scenes his expression of joy turns to dejection as he espies his father standing in the rear of the theater. The final lines of the play are prophetic. Puck, or Robin Goodfellow, worker of magic spells and childish pranks, apologizes to the audience: "If we shadows have offended, / Think but this, and all is mended, / That you have but slumbered here / While these visions did appear. . . ." Neil, too, apologizes. He apologizes for what his father has seen, only a dream of his son's making.

The line separating reality from dreams, however, has become blurred for the adolescent. When the curtain falls, friends and teachers try to congratulate Neil on his performance, but his father shuffles him home. There, he sits in a chair in his father's study as his father informs him of his future—he will be taken out of Welton and enrolled in a military school—and his mother weeps silently in the shadows. Shot from a high angle, Neil appears small and defeated, defeated by his father's dominance. Neil clings to the dream, however; "I was good, I was really good," he says to himself as he sits alone.

The dream, too, has defeated the character. Like Icarus, he has discovered passion and energy, but he knows no bounds. He has flown too close to the sun, and his wings have melted. As his parents prepare for bed, his father carefully aligning his slippers next to the bed and bizarrely placing a machete on the nightstand, Neil also prepares for the day's end. In his room he readies himself for the sacrifice. With the deliberate pace of a ritual, he removes his shirt, opens the windows, and ceremonially dons the wreath he wore as Puck. As the cold winter air blows against him, he appears to recapture the joy he felt earlier. Rather than yield, he sacrifices himself to the dream and to the ideal of living an extraordinary life. Moments later, he shoots himself.

Neil has experienced the ordeal of adolescence but has not passed safely to adulthood. He has not succeeded in integrating his aspirations and ambitions into his true self, and his suicide does not surprise viewers. At least two of the other students, however, emerge victorious from the struggle. Knox Overstreet (Josh Charles) and Todd Anderson (Ethan Hawke) both discover new desires and dreams, and begin to integrate them into their personalities. Knox discovers romance and against considerable odds gets his girl in the end. Todd, who has lived in the shadow of an overachieving older brother and who has been scarred by the indifference and shallow materialism of his parents, overcomes a nearly paralyzing fear of speaking and expressing his feelings. The character of Neil, however, is the most compelling. As an individual personality, he sends plenty of signals that emotionally he is in trouble, and Robert Sean Leonard's portrayal of the character is quite convincing.

In *The Madness of King George*, George III's recognition of his private self as distinct from his public self is regarded as a sign of recovery from mental illness. Is the corollary that an inability to distinguish the private from the public self, or appropriate from inappropriate behavior according to social standards, thus a sign of mental illness?

Several movies have dealt well with this difficulty of establishing a uniform standard or definition of mental health. One of the best is *A Woman under the Influence* (1974), directed by John Cassavetes. The story focuses on Mabel Longetti (Gena Rowlands), who drifts in and out of control, and the efforts of her husband, Nick (Peter Falk), a city maintenance worker, to cope with her behavior. A hallmark of Mabel's behavior is her inability to distinguish private self from public self. As a result, she often behaves in ways that other people label as inappropriate.

During the rising action of the story, Mabel is seen waiting for the school bus to drop off her children. Impatient and filled with nervous energy because she has planned a party for them, she has no watch and no idea what time it is. Frantically gyrating about, up and down the sidewalk, she attempts to get the time from a passerby. First one woman, and then another, ignore her request. Clearly they want nothing to do with her. Her odd costume, which mixes an upswept hairdo and provocatively short skirt with little-girl pink socks, and her loud, abrasive manner do not invite polite conversation or even civil response from these strangers, dressed in their tidy, mix-and-match coordinates. They do their best to ignore her presence.

A later episode underscores Mabel's inability to conform. After working all night on a water main break, Nick brings his crew home for breakfast. As usual on these occasions, Mabel cooks spaghetti, and the crowd of a dozen or so congregate at the dining room table. Characteristically, Mabel's concentration wanes, and she wanders back and forth between being engaged in the social gathering and carrying on a conversation with herself. One of Nick's older, Italian buddies begins singing opera, and Mabel, who loves opera, rises from the table, listening and watching with a childlike interest. Another buddy sings, even more impressively, and Mabel moves right up to his face, declaring him "handsome" and saying "I love this face." She doesn't seem to know when enough is enough, and she repeats her declarations several times. She then wants to dance with the fellows. Nick, who has become visibly uncomfortable with her too-familiar, flirtatious behavior, says that's enough and orders her to sit down. At one point when Mabel is moving from one person to another, the camera captures a shot of the "PRIVATE" sign posted on the bathroom door to the rear of the dining room. The sign is poised just above her head.

Mabel's behavior cannot, however, within the context of the film be neatly labeled as inappropriate. Nick, to whom Mabel consistently looks for reassurance, describes his wife as "unusual," "not crazy." Mabel's behavior is even mirrored several times in Nick's behavior.

A notable parallel occurs involving their children. As Mabel careens to a complete mental collapse and the story toward its climax, one of her fears is that she is a bad mother. The party she had planned for her children ends in a debacle. As Nick and his mother, Margaret, burst in on the scene, they find an unknown male—in fact, the father of two children invited to the party—in the children's bedroom with Mabel, trying to collect them, half-clad in pirate costumes, and get them out of the house. Nick and Mabel's youngest child, Maria, is running through the house naked. Margaret, who at times is quite critical of her daughter-in-law's behavior, cries in shock and disbelief, "This kid is naked." Her exaggerated reaction borders on the comic, however, and Cassavetes is expressing the film's judgment against such rigid parental authority and adherence to conventional mores.

By the end of this episode, Mabel is hysterical and begins to have a seizure. Nick can no longer cope. Earlier he had scuffled with Harold Jensen, the visiting father, and began drinking heavily. Finally, he has Mabel hospitalized. The following day, he and one of his work buddies take the children to the beach. Like Mabel, he worries about his performance as a parent; he says to his buddy that he feels he doesn't know his kids. Like Mabel earlier, when he goes to the school to get the children, he is without a watch and frantic to know the time. His inability to deal with Mabel's condition and their plight finally gets the best of his judgment, and by the end of the day he has fed the kids beer and brought them home wobbly and too tired to do anything but go to sleep. Even in 1974, before media attention was being given to the problem of youngsters and alcohol, his behavior causes viewers to wonder who poses the greatest risk for the kids, mommy or daddy.

In the end, Mabel and Nick prevail in their chaotic unconventionality. The evening that Mabel returns from the hospital, a visit with both families parallels the earlier scene that is the movie's climax. This time, however, when her feelings are out of control, she and Nick manage to cope, affirming their love for and acceptance of one another.

In one of Hollywood's most sympathetic portrayals of the mentally ill, *One Flew over the Cuckoo's Nest* (1975), directed by Milos Forman, showcases the demands social institutions place on the individual to conform. Adapted by Lawrence Hauben and Bo Goldman from Ken Kesey's novel, the screenplay, like the book and the concepts of R. D. Laing, raises the questions of what is normal behavior and what is madness. Furthermore, when society attempts to impose a false self, a socially acceptable mode of behavior, on an individual, then who is mad, the individual who does not or cannot conform or the persons who seek to impose their standards?

Forman's film accents the boundaries used to separate the insane from the sane by drawing a strong "us" versus "them" contrast. When the central character, felon R. P. McMurphy (Jack Nicholson), is admitted to the state mental hospital for observation, a long shot establishes the conflict. As he is escorted by hospital authorities and law officers down a long, starkly white corridor to the men's ward, he dances fey-like and mockingly to the music that plays most of the day on the ward. To McMurphy, the scene is pure comedy; he is amused at the situation into which he has landed. To the grim-faced escorts, however, his behavior is evidence of why he is being admitted in the first place.

The contrast of insane versus sane, us versus them, dominates the film. The patients are a band of misfits to the staff, set off by their hospital gowns and herded around like so many sheep. In actuality, they are a cross section of humanity: the dwarfish Martini (Danny DeVito), who smiles incessantly; the immense Chief (Will Sampson), who does not speak; the squat, bespectacled Cheswick (Sydney Lassick); the gawdy, agog Taber (Christopher Lloyd); the supercilious Harding (William Redfield); and, most poignantly, the fragile young Billy (Brad Dourif), whose painful stutter constantly reminds viewers of the isolation the character feels from the rest of the world, that world represented here by the hospital staff. The staff on the ward are led by Nurse Mildred Ratched (Louise Fletcher), an untouchable if ever there was one in her crisp white uniform, starched cap, and rigid hairdo and demeanor. The clerks in their white shirts and black bow ties are a comical but also menacing blend of soda jerk, cop, and prison guard. They are present to light the men's cigarettes, escort them to their baths, and maintain the polite semblance of a garden party. They also quickly move in on the group, like bouncers in a bar scuffle, whenever a hint of trouble arises.

The staff keeps a comfortable distance from these misfits, and it is fear on both sides that maintains the distance. The patients comply with the rules and regulations of the ward, out of fear of reprisal from Nurse Ratched. Like inmates in a prison, they can lose various privileges if they break the rules. When McMurphy spits into Harding's face the capsule he has concealed in his mouth rather than swallowed, underscoring that no one can force him to take medication, Harding says, "That wasn't smart. She [Ratched] could've seen you."

Nurse Ratched's ability to threaten and punish can be quite sinister. She plays on the patients' fear of people in the outside world. In group therapy she antagonizes Harding and other patients by reminding them of what their wives, mothers, and others have confided in her. In the film's climax, she drives Billy into a tragic frenzy with the image of his domineering mother, who presumably will exert some unspoken punishment on him after Ratched reports his behavior to her.

The men are indeed afraid of crossing Nurse Ratched. The workers fear the patients, too. In one scene, when no one is in the front office of the nurses' station, McMurphy slips in to turn down the volume of the music, which is driving even him, someone who is generally comfortable amid chaos and noise, crazy. The nurse assistant appears from the backroom and screams in visible fear at being face-to-face with one of the patients.

One Flew over the Cuckoo's Nest seeks to answer the questions McMurphy asks: What is meant by crazy? Who is crazy here? The sole purpose of the plot is for Dr. Spivey (Dean R. Brooks) and his staff to determine whether McMurphy is mentally ill or should be sent back to the work farm. In the opening interview with the patient, Dr. Spivey summarizes McMurphy's criminal record, which includes five arrests for assault. McMurphy replies that, yes, he's had five fights, but then Rocky Marciano has had forty and he's a millionaire. Mac's point, obviously, is that madness might just be a matter of perception. The difficulty of defining it is exacerbated by the unreliability of what is observed. Dr. Spivey tells McMurphy that the prison officials think Mac has been faking craziness in order to get out of work detail. How can the doctor evaluate the patient, when the patient's behavior is not real? Like Hamlet feigning madness, McMurphy defies evaluation by any conventional medical criteria.

Real madness, fake madness, and the problem in perception that they present are demonstrated deftly in a scene shared by McMurphy and the Chief. The moment is a footnote on a group therapy session that has just transpired and in which McMurphy learns that most of the men on the ward are there voluntarily. He is stunned. "What are you doing here?" he asks Billy. "You're not crazy." In fact, he tells the group, they are "no crazier than the average asshole walking around out there on the streets." His disbelief provokes a general questioning by the men of the ward's rules, then a brawl incited by Ratched's confiscation earlier of the men's cigarettes, and finally Cheswick, the Chief, and McMurphy all being subjected to electroshock therapy for their part in the rebellion. As Mac and the Chief wait their turn outside the treatment room, Mac offers his fellow inmate a piece of gum, to which the deafmute replies, "Thank-you." After a few seconds, it hits McMurphy: the Chief isn't mute, or deaf. Mac is ecstatic by the con the Chief has pulled off: "You fooled 'em all."

The Chief's revelation is not the first time the men are able to relate to McMurphy and in the process break out of their quiet compliance with ward routine. As the plot progresses Mac becomes a coach and mentor, a doctor of sorts, among the patients. In group therapy, which Ratched conducts like a legal proceeding—"You've stated on more than one occasion," she says to Harding—Mac gives them the courage to question, raise their voices, even express their frustrations. When Ratched fights Mac's suggestion that they be allowed to watch the World Series on television, Cheswick, following Mac's earlier lead, challenges her judgment, asserting—albeit timidly—that the activity would be a type of therapy. Mac's ability to offer other kinds of expression climaxes as he sits in front of the silent television, apparently defeated by Ratched's power, demonstrated by her refusal to let them watch the game. In defiance of her rules and her lack of imagination, he is able to imagine the game. His shouts and calls to the invisible players are so believable that the other men are drawn to the television. In seconds they, too, are spectators at a World Series game, hooting and cheering, defying the perceptions and lack of perceptiveness of Nurse Ratched.

In its portrayal of mental illness and the treatment of mental illness, *One Flew over the Cuckoo's Nest* remains a classic. Although more is learned about mental illness every day, difficulties in diagnosing it in its various forms and treating it remain. The movie is still criticized by some mental health practitioners and advocates for its negative portrayal of psychiatrists and psychiatric hospitals and therefore for its contribution to the continuing stigmatization of mental illness (Carter 230). Those negative portrayals, however, are not without basis in fact, as evidenced in the many narratives written by and about mental patients (Jones, "Literature and Medicine: Narratives of Mental Illness"). In *Darkness Visible: A Memoir of Madness*, William Styron's 1990 personal account of depression, the prize-winning American novelist expresses disdain for several aspects of his treatment: his doctor's reckless prescription of Halcion, a powerful tranquilizer (49, 70–71); his doctor's bias against hospitalization (67–68); and hospital activities such as group therapy and art therapy (73–75).

One Flew over the Cuckoo's Nest indeed dramatizes and condemns the abuses of patients that were prevalent in many hospitals throughout much of the twentieth century. Electroconvulsive therapy (ECT) and psychosurgery both are used in the story not to treat illness but to control people. Such misuse, while difficult to view, was, nonetheless, possible during the time period. The movie also highlights the dilemma in which both patient and doctor sometimes find themselves. Dr. Spivey in Forman's film is tentative in his evaluation of McMurphy, and Mabel's doctor in *A Woman under the Influence* seems powerless to manage her care. In both cases, the portrayals help show the difficulties that attend mental illness and its diagnosis and treatment.

Like other movies discussed in this chapter, *Nuts* (1987), directed by Martin Ritt, concerns the false self and definitions of madness. Like *A Woman under the Influence* and *One Flew over the Cuckoo's Nest*, *Nuts* asks questions for which there are not always clear answers: What is meant by the word *crazy*? Who can be called crazy? In this movie the protagonist refuses to conform to others' expectations and standards, and she is therefore labeled insane.

On the surface, Claudia Faith Draper (Barbra Streisand) seems to be "nuts." She is belligerent, she trusts no one, and, typical of the stereotype of the mentally ill, she becomes violent when she is provoked. When the film opens she is locked up in the psychiatric ward of the New York County Prison Hospital. In hospital gown and shower slippers she is led to a courtroom where, viewers learn, she has been charged with first-degree manslaughter. The lawyer hired by her parents, however, has entered a motion that she be declared incompetent to stand trial, and a psychiatric report supports that conclusion. When neither her lawyer nor the judge will acknowledge her pleas that she is innocent, she physically attacks the attorney. With his unceremonious departure—it seems his nose has been broken—the judge appoints Aaron Levinsky (Richard Dreyfuss) from Legal Aid as her attorney. Having witnessed his new client's refusal to be called incompetent, Levinsky, played with an intelligence, charm, and self-effacing manner that make him hard for even Claudia to dislike, challenges the motion, at least until he can consult with her.

The story tells of the ensuing competency hearing. Flashbacks and other devices tell the audience of Claudia's life before the action of the movie—as a child and adolescent from a well-to-do home, as a respectable wife, and most recently as a high-priced call girl. The flashbacks are effective in not only presenting the essential facts of her life but also showing the kind of woman she is, intelligent and sophisticated as well as private and mistrustful. Levinsky's visit to her Manhattan apartment gives additional insight, revealing a sitting room/office that is curtained off from the rest of the apartment and that seems to preserve the best parts of her childhood through photos of her parents, a Raggedy Ann doll perched on the mantel, and other toys. A dream she has shows the event for which she has been charged with manslaughter, actually a clear case of self-defense against a client who turned ugly and violent.

Claudia endures condescending treatment from nearly everyone involved in the hearing. Frequently she is discussed as though she is not present or she is referred to as a girl, even though she is well into her thirties. The prison psychiatrist, Dr. Morrison, refers to her as "a sick girl," her stepfather calls her "a very disturbed girl," and the judge addresses her as "young lady." When she is to testify, the judge is willing to make a special allowance: she need not go to the witness stand but may testify from the table where she is seated with her attorney. Claudia's reply is curt: "I'm not an invalid." She also assures him, "I'm not gonna hurt you."

Psychiatrists get the brunt of the film's criticism of attitudes toward mental illness. Dr. Morrison is arrogant and presumptuous. Perfectly realized in the performance of Eli Wallach, the doctor responds to the patient by being amused or smugly judgmental. Too early in their contact for him to know about her life, he tells her with authority that he is there to help her put her life in order. He also has gotten comfortable with the routine chores of describing symptoms and making diagnoses. He testifies that, in his opinion, she cannot stand trial because she believes there's a conspiracy to lock her up. Indeed, she talks to him about "some guys

[who] are trying to put me away"—and her father, for one, would like to see her in a hospital for the criminally insane. The psychiatrist, however, cannot separate her reality from his textbook theory because he does not know her. In addition, his colleague does not speak English well enough to carry on a conversation with her. When Claudia refers to the pair as Fric and Frac, she is not making a cheap joke.

The inadequacy of labels and definitions is a steady theme in the film. Although he believes Claudia is "disturbed" and "troubled," Dr. Morrison says, "*Crazy* is a word I dislike." He might as well use the word, however, because his diagnosis of her as incompetent is based on appearances and behavior that he does not understand. Appearances are not a sure indicator: take the example of Dr. Johnson, another inmate/patient in the New York County Prison Hospital. She looks and talks the part of a medical professional, so when Claudia introduces her to Levinsky, implying she is a psychiatrist, he believes his client. When Dr. Johnson stands and he sees her hospital gown, he is disbelieving. "She looks so normal," he says to Claudia. As far as looks and conduct go, Levinsky has an aunt on Long Island, he tells the prosecutor, who is crazier than Claudia Draper, and she is the president of the PTA.

Levinsky is not surprised at his capacity to be fooled; labels do fool people. Unlike the doctors and the other lawyers in the movie, he is open to and tolerant of the atypical in human behavior. He acts as an eye through which viewers see Claudia and sympathize with her. Back in her hospital room, after the climactic testimony of her stepfather, she tells Levinsky she is afraid. He responds, "Don't be afraid. You're sane." Their shared ability to accept the sometimes bizarre ways that humans respond to pain and hurt confirms what Claudia has said all along.

As the story unfolds, viewers come to accept what Claudia and Levinsky—and finally the judge—know. Claudia is "ill mannered" and "irritating," and "she disturbs the peace," Levinsky sums up for the judge. She is even emotionally disturbed; being sexually abused by her stepfather left her deeply, emotionally damaged, frightened and withdrawn from humanity. She might not be normal in that she refuses to conform to socially prescribed roles. She is not incompetent, however, to stand trial; she understands the charge against her and she can assist in her defense. Nor is she crazy. In fact, she is not only cognizant of the reality around her but also insightful in interpreting and adjusting to it.

In the film's concluding scene, Claudia marches triumphantly from the courtroom, and then viewers see her walking joyfully down a busy, crowded New York street. She passes a man dressed in a gaudy shirt, talking and singing boisterously, to no one. She turns around, looks again, and smiles confidently.

A number of other movies that have treated the subject of mental illness have explored the struggle of the individual against conformity. Graeme Clifford's 1982 box-office hit, *Frances*, depicts the struggle of early film and stage actress Frances Farmer against her mother's will as well as her struggle against the Hollywood establishment. Jane Campion's *An Angel at My Table* (1990) chronicles the life of New Zealand writer Janet Frame, who battled social conventions and expectations to find her own voice and express her vision. Both films spend considerable time showing the cruel conditions and practices that dominated mental hospitals in the 1930s. Neither movie, however, is in content or theme concerned with mental illness, and neither explores it as a human condition. In *Frances*, the protagonist is not diagnosed as mentally ill; her mother has her hospitalized to confine and control her and to try to coerce her to change her behavior. In *An Angel at My Table*, Frame is misdiagnosed as schizophrenic. In each movie the attention given to the practices and conditions of mental hospitals is misleading and superfluous to the central conflict, tending to exploit viewers' fears of mental illness and failing to provide insight on the protagonist's dilemma.

The pressure to conform is pervasive. Conforming to social standards, expectations, and mores is often a survival technique. Sometimes, the struggle against those demands results in a divided or false self that threatens the individual's psychic and emotional well-being. Movies about that struggle give viewers perspectives not only on mental illness but on the human desire to be free and true to self.

~

CHAPTER TWO

The Denial of Reality

An alternative to reality has always appealed to humans. Whether knowingly or not, people through the ages have chosen a dream, an illusion, or simply forgetfulness rather than face reality. People will cling to a dream long after the evidence indicates they should let go. Every day millions of Americans bear out this truth when they buy what they hope will be winning lottery tickets. The desire to deny or forget the reality in favor of a more positive or less fearsome alternative is one that most people can understand. It should be no surprise that this desire or need is sometimes at the root of mental illness or at least a contributing factor.

One of the earliest films to deal exclusively with mental illness, *The Snake Pit*, draws on Mary Jane Ward's inability to deal with events in her childhood, chronicled in her book of the same title. Directed by Anatole Litvak and produced in 1948, the movie tells the story of Virginia Stewart Cunningham (Olivia de Havilland), who has experienced a breakdown and is hospitalized in a state facility. As the plot progresses, viewers learn that Virginia unconsciously harbors guilt over the death of her father when she was just a child. That guilt has troubled her adulthood, affecting her relationships with men and creating bouts of anxiety and depression. The movie reflects an understanding of mental illness that informed viewers of today can accept.

The protagonist's inability to face painful realities of her past is posited as a major contributing cause of her illness, but the story also asserts that the causes of mental illness are sometimes complex and not totally identified and understood.

The title and the image conjured by the title no doubt helped give *The Snake Pit* its "original shock value" (Maltin 1290). That the movie stirred the public in 1948 is supported by the fact that "the British censor insisted on a foreword explaining that everyone in the film was an actor and that conditions in British mental hospitals were unlike those depicted" (Halliwell 933). *The Snake Pit* is, however, a remarkably realistic portrayal of mental illness. More than fifty years later, it is still one of the most sensitive and sympathetic portrayals of mental illness to have come out of Hollywood.

First, the point of view throughout the film is that of the central character. The movie opens with a shot of dappled sunlight on sycamore trees in a parklike setting. Virginia, who sits on what appears to be a park bench, is confused and disheveled. The voice-over is of her thoughts and bits of conversations as she tries to figure out where she is and who belongs to the voices she hears. Through Virginia's perspective, viewers witness the sense of isolation the patient experiences. Later in the opening sequence, when she reenters the hospital building with the dozens of other women who have been milling about on the grounds, she is still trying to determine where she is. Seeing the bars and locked doors of the ward, she speculates, first, that she is visiting a zoo and, then, that she is in a prison. Throughout her hospital stay, she is quite aware of her separateness from the healthy portion of society. She remarks to her husband, Robert (Mark Stevens), during one of his visits that keeping doors locked seems to be the most important thing to the staff—that is, keeping the patients separate from the rest of the world. Her remark brings to mind what Michel Foucault theorized to be the driving force behind the development of mental hospitals. In *Madness and Civilization* he brilliantly examines the origin of the asylum in eighteenth-century Europe as an effort not only to isolate the mentally ill but to maintain power over them.

Virginia also feels her separateness from the other patients, and this point is important because it accents her individuality as well as theirs. In this regard the movie is well ahead of its time. Virginia carefully observes the other patients and repeatedly assesses her perceptions and behavior in comparison with theirs. She is not just one more mad-woman, indistinguishable from the others. In fact, even in her confusion, she is witty, intelligent, and likable.

The image from which the movie's title is taken is Virginia's metaphor for Ward 33, where some of the hospital's most severely ill women are housed. Virginia is confined there in a straitjacket after an episode in which fear and paranoia have left her out of control. Ward 33 is a bedlam of sights and sounds, as patients pace about, some acting out delusions, others nearly hysterical. From images of the individual women the movie cuts to a long shot from above, and the ward metamorphoses into a pit, the tiny human figures appearing to writhe in its depths. Virginia recognizes that the image is an illusion, that the ward only seems like a snake pit. The image, she tells her doctor, actually comes from something she once read, a primitive theory that, if being thrown into a snake pit could drive a sane person insane, then perhaps the same treatment might shock an insane person back to sanity. She also knows that neither she nor the other patients in the ward are monsters. They are human beings, they have names and personalities, and she forms warm friendships with some of them.

Second, even those elements that have the potential to exploit the poor conditions of mental asylums are desensationalized. The treatment Virginia receives illustrates the point. Most notable is the electroshock, or electroconvulsive, therapy (ECT) that is administered. The brutal nature of this still controversial treatment is emphasized in the moments leading to its administration. Virginia is led to a bed, mandated to lie down, and surrounded by a cadre of nurses who hold her down. The conductant is applied to her temples and as the switch is hit, the musical score crescendos and screams. The scene is repeated several times. During the treatments, however, the camera never focuses on Virginia's face. She is confused and she is frightened: is her crime so great, she wonders, that she should be electrocuted? But the camera does not exploit her fear. It is also made clear that her doctor orders the therapy only "to establish contact" with her and she does not complete the full course of treatments because she begins to show improvement by communicating with him and others.

Unlike some later films, such as *One Flew over the Cuckoo's Nest*, where ECT is used to discipline and control patients, *The Snake Pit* depicts ECT as a treatment of last resort for people who are severely depressed. By reputable physicians it has been so regarded since the late 1930s, when it was introduced in this country.

Virginia's psychiatrist is also depicted sympathetically. To a small degree Dr. Kik (Leo Genn) is a stereotype: when he consults with Virginia in his office, he pauses to fill his pipe; not coincidentally, on the wall behind the physician, whose preferred method of treatment is psychotherapy, hangs what appears to be a portrait of Sigmund Freud. But it is only on the surface that he fits later stereotypes of the aloof, questioning, note-taking psychiatrist. Although Virginia complains that she knows nothing about him and he knows everything about her, sincerity and humanity dominate the character. One of the least sympathetically drawn of the hospital staff, the head nurse of Ward 1, resents patients like Virginia because she is what the nurse calls one of Dr. Kik's special cases. Viewers are given enough details to believe that Virginia's doctor treats each of his patients as individual and therefore as special.

Like Dr. Kik, most of the hospital's staff are compassionate and caring. Nurses know patients by first name, and there are numerous instances of a nurse gently taking a patient by the shoulders and comforting or otherwise helping her. As with Dr. Kik, certain details emphasize the separateness of the patients from the staff. The nurses are meticulously—almost annoyingly so—coiffed and attired in crisply starched white uniforms. Their manner, however, is not cold or tormenting. They do not take pleasure in keeping the patients locked up or in carrying out other duties. Rather, the film presents them in almost documentary fashion, going about their business of caring for the patients according to procedures prevailing at the time.

Juniper Hill State Hospital, the main setting of the movie, has the outward form of the large, impersonal state-run institution. Virginia is confused when she initially thinks she is in prison, but the similarities in the appearance of the two types of institutions help justify her conclusion. Before the advent of community-based treatment centers in the 1960s, state hospitals, like prisons, were built to accommodate large numbers of people. At one meeting of administrators and doctors, the film documents for viewers the overcrowded conditions at Juniper Hill.

Some areas of the hospital, viewers are told, have more than twice the number of patients they were designed to house, and the numbers are growing daily, even while funds remain insufficient. The head of the hospital wants Dr. Kik to understand that, although some of the doctors and staff may seem uncaring about individual patients, even overeager to discharge them, the sheer realities of the numbers force them to move patients along.

All of that said, it must be acknowledged that the movie does play on some fears about mental illness and mental hospitals. One of those fears is the suspicion that it is a thin line separating sanity from madness and the closely related notion that, like leprosy, madness might be contagious. One of the patients on Ward 33 is a Miss Summerfield, who was once the head nurse of Ward 1 and who still thinks she is a psychiatric nurse. Asylum staff-gone-mad is a standard ingredient of horror movies.

One of the master strokes of the portrait *The Snake Pit* paints is the long, slow recovery process that accompanies mental illness. Virginia achieves mental health through a variety of treatments, including ice baths and hypnosis in addition to ECT and psychotherapy, and with the help of a patient and intelligent psychiatrist who does not subscribe to easy fixes. The closing sequences bring the movie full circle by emphasizing that the gulf between Virginia and others has been closed. At a social gathering for patients and their visitors, a member of the staff— or perhaps a patient, it is not clear—sings a poignant interpretation of "Going Home." As the camera pans the faces of the patients, who have stopped talking and moved toward the stage to listen, viewers appreciate their need, the basic human need, to belong, rather than to be isolated and separate. The need to rejoin the larger group is a theme of some later films that treat mental illness, but no film handles it as touchingly as Litvak's.

In *The Snake Pit*, the protagonist's anxiety, depression, and eventual collapse result, at least in part, from her denial of reality—her father's death and her sense of guilt about it. In the 1950s another very effective depiction of mental illness dealt with what is generally considered to be a more extreme denial of reality, the phenomenon known as multiple personality. *The Three Faces of Eve* (1957) tells the true story of one of the first documented cases of this condition.

Nunnally Johnson, who directed and produced the film, also wrote the screenplay from the book of the same title by Corbett H. Thigpen, M.D., and Hervey M. Cleckley, M.D. The cause of the patient's multiple personality is not entirely explained. Early in the diagnosis Dr. Luther (Lee J. Cobb), the psychiatrist, laments to his partner, Dr. Day, that the patient, Eve (Joanne Woodward), seems to have had an "abnormally normal childhood," and it would be more convenient for her doctor if a single traumatic event could be uncovered as the cause of her illness. As the story unfolds, Eve's mother emerges as a major cause of Eve's condition. Her mother, it seems, had some old-fashioned and misguided ideas about child rearing. In the only significant flashback to her childhood, Eve remembers the trauma of being forced by her mother to kiss the face of her grandmother's corpse resting in its coffin. The implication is that the experience was not an isolated one but part of a pattern with which even Eve's father was uncomfortable.

The film is more concerned, however, with showing the illness and the confusion and pain the patient undergoes than with identifying and understanding causes. Like *Now, Voyager*, *The Snake Pit*, and other sensitive films on the subject, *The Three Faces of Eve* appreciates the complexity of mental illness. Often, it cannot be understood in terms of a single cause, nor is it based in purely biological or purely environmental factors.

The Three Faces of Eve emphasizes this complexity. As the first film to present multiple personality—now called by clinicians dissociative identity disorder (*Diagnostic and Statistical Manual of Mental Disorders* 526)—Johnson's movie portrays not only the confusion of the patient but also the struggle of her doctors to diagnose and treat a condition that is new to them. The movie has a documentary feel. Narrated by Alistair Cooke, it begins by chronicling the early symptoms of the patient's condition and the first occurrences of unusual behavior, as witnessed by her husband, Ralph (David Wayne). The movie then traces the progress and treatment of the illness, carefully providing chronological markers in the telling. It might be more accurate to say the movie lifts a veil that conceals the truth from all parties. As the psychiatrists and the patient come to recognize and understand aspects of the illness, so do the viewers.

In Eve's case the medical community seems as baffled as the patient. The doctors admit they have never encountered a case of multiple personality. In a couple of instances their honesty provides wry humor. For example, they struggle clumsily to find a language to discuss the case. When the third personality reveals herself, the doctors attempt to learn exactly who she is. In questioning her, Dr. Day asks, "How long have you been around?"—observing midsentence that "It's not easy to phrase these questions without sounding like an idiot."

Following the 1976 television movie *Sybil*, which told another purportedly true story of a woman with multiple personality, there was a spate of other supposedly actual accounts, covered by the popular press and television talk shows (Milstone). In the 1980s and early 1990s, television viewers may have come to suspect that any of their neighbors might be harboring two or three or even dozens of other personalities. Multiple personality seemed to have been reaching epidemic numbers. In the 1950s the disorder was rare, as *The Three Faces of Eve* makes clear. The accuracy of the dramatic increase in cases in recent decades is still being debated (*Diagnostic* 528).

In its documentary style the film avoids sensationalizing the illness. The treatment presented in *The Three Faces of Eve* is plainly psychoanalytic. Eve is hospitalized, but only for two weeks for further observation after the doctors have diagnosed her condition. The hospital seems no different from a general acute care facility: there are no bars, no locked doors, no straitjackets. Eve's treatment primarily consists of talk therapy, dream analysis, and some hypnosis. Shock treatment and medications are not mentioned, and viewers assume those are not part of the treatment.

For readers who have not seen the movie, it is helpful to describe the three personalities. Eve White, the patient who presents herself to Dr. Luther, is a young housewife—compliant, prudishly modest, and bland to the point of being "dreary," to use Dr. Day's description of her. Eve Black, the first of the other personalities to emerge, is an unmarried playgirl—fun loving to the point of being reckless, and uninhibited in her behavior and self-expression. Jane, the third personality, is a pleasant young woman who has no memory of the other two personalities but is able to behave as a responsible mother and citizen. The narrator labels all three personalities "incomplete" and asks what it is that nature may have intended this woman, Eve White/Eve Black/Jane, to be. Freud himself could not have designed a better textbook case. As Jane, the ego, becomes stronger, she integrates those parts of Eve White, the superego, and Eve Black, the id, that make her whole and healthy. The integration is described as the death of the two Eve's. With the integration Jane also gains memory of the self that goes back to childhood.

The Three Faces of Eve is intent on portraying the complexity of the illness. The film ends happily but only after a hard-fought battle. Two years after Jane "survives," she and her new husband, Earl, are finally re-united with her daughter, who has been in the care of her parents. Like The Snake Pit, this movie ends on the theme of going home, as Jane writes to her doctor that she, Earl, and Bonnie are at last "going home together." Recovery, like diagnosis, is not a quick or easy process.

Eve/Jane's first husband, it should be noted, had divorced her much earlier when she was receiving treatment. Her condition and the stigma of mental illness were more than the unsophisticated, unedu-cated Ralph could handle. He had managed to stay with his wife as long as he did because he clung to Dr. Luther's comment that Eve was not "crazy." That comment is correct if crazy is defined as out of touch with reality. The person with multiple personality has not departed from re-ality, but has adapted to it in an extraordinary way. For at least a while, Ralph could deal with Eve's condition because she—and he—had not been strapped with the label.

Mental health legislation in this country had helped to boost awareness of mental illness by 1957, and several other movies pro-duced in the 1950s treated or featured the subject, interestingly if not as effectively as The Three Faces of Eve and the earlier Snake Pit. Rain-tree County (1957), directed by Edward Dmytryk, attempts the epic sweep of Gone with the Wind but is flawed by its Gothic and macabre elements. Nearly three hours long, the movie tells the story of John Shawnessy, a bookish but handsome Yankee who marries Susannah Drake, a lovely but disturbed Southern belle. Tricking John into mar-riage by pretending to be pregnant, Susannah usurps the place of Nell Gaither, Johnny's childhood friend, school chum, and soul mate. No-ble, introspective John is played by Montgomery Clift; dark, brooding Susannah is played by Elizabeth Taylor; and sunny, wholesome Nell is played by blonde beauty Eva Marie Saint. The story takes place chiefly in Freehaven, Indiana, in Raintree County, as well as the South in the years just before and during the Civil War.

Like Virginia Cunningham and Eve White, Susannah cannot face reality. She is haunted by the past, troubled by dreams and insomnia, and confused about actual events. As a child of nine, she survived the fire that destroyed her family's plantation and killed her parents and Henrietta, the black woman who took care of her. Henrietta, Susannah insists to John, was not a slave, but, as Susannah later realized, the mistress whom her father brought to the plantation from Cuba. One of the dolls the adult Susannah insists on keeping on her bed is a doll that burned in the fire. Much of her behavior is motivated by guilt and self-hatred because of the role she believes she played in the fire. She especially feels guilt for having loved Henrietta more than her own mother, who, according to a cousin, was not able to care for Susannah because she, the mother, was insane. Underlying Susannah's guilt and self-loathing is an intense phobia about "Negro blood." She has convinced herself that she is actually Henrietta's child. When Susannah gives birth to a son, she thinks there were two babies, one of them "dark" and perhaps discarded.

Taylor plays the role of Susannah with the melodramatic angst of a Brontë or Dickens character. Confusion and paranoia finally lead her to run away with her son to the area in the South where she grew up. John, no longer strapped with a wife and child, signs up with the Union army, which conveniently takes him to where Susannah can be found. And find her, Johnny does, in an asylum, portrayed in keeping with conditions that were still quite possible in the mid-1860s. Some of the inmates are in cages, others are in chains, and there is plenty of screaming and gnashing of teeth. Luckily, Susannah is, as the attendant explains, "normal enough now" and surprisingly coherent in spite of the surroundings. Her hair has been chopped off and her skirt hoops apparently closeted, but her eye liner is intact. When John says he wants to take her home, he uses the word *normal* and she responds, "Normal—I've come to love the sound of that word." Viewers wonder where and how she gained that insight, certainly not at the facility where she is being kept as nothing more than an animal. John does take her home to Raintree County; he truly loves her. Her guilt, now extending to a belief that she has ruined her husband's life, cannot be assuaged, however, and her suicidal tendencies triumph.

Raintree County is weakened by its melodrama, but the character of Susannah wins viewers' sympathy. Her inability to face the past precludes any possibility for emotional stability, true love, and happiness. Viewers sympathize because Susannah cannot help herself, nor can her husband help her. In addition, since there was no effective treatment for mental illness at the time, her death is accepted as inevitable.

A more effective and realistic 1950s portrayal of madness again features Elizabeth Taylor as the emotionally ill heroine. *Suddenly, Last Summer* (1959), directed by Joseph Mankiewicz, is based on the play by Tennessee Williams and was written for the screen by Williams and Gore Vidal. The setting of the story is 1937, Lions View State Asylum, a dilapidated, overcrowded state-run hospital in New Orleans, its steel and brick-and-mortar construction suggesting a prison or military barracks more than a health care facility. Oddly contrasted with this setting is the newest addition to the hospital's staff, young Dr. John Cukrowicz (Montgomery Clift) of Chicago, a pioneer in psychosurgery, namely, lobotomy, an operation considered experimental. Enter Mrs. Violet Venable (Katharine Hepburn), the wealthy widow who promises the hospital director a $1 million building dedicated to psychosurgery and donated in memory of her son, Sebastian. The catch is that Mrs. Venable needs help with an "urgent" family problem, treatment of her insane niece, Catherine Holly (Taylor).

The name Mrs. Venable uses for Catherine's condition is "dementia praecox," a term for schizophrenia that actually was out of date by 1937. When Dr. Cukrowicz asks for a more specific description, she speaks of her niece's fits of violence, delusions, and babbling. Some of this babbling she characterizes as obscene because it concerns her son's death the previous summer in a remote village near Amalfi, an event that Catherine witnessed but cannot remember. Violet's wish is that the doctor perform a lobotomy on Catherine and thereby exorcise her demons.

Lobotomy had been developed and first used in the mid-1930s as a way of controlling violent behavior in the mentally ill, but by the late 1940s the negative effects of the operation were being seen. Often it left patients emotionless. By 1959, when *Suddenly, Last Summer* was produced, advances in medications made lobotomy unnecessary except in the most violent cases. Dr. Cukrowicz reflects this contemporary, cautious position of the mental health community when he tells Violet that the operation is only for the "unapproachable," the hopeless, because it carries significant risks for the patient and its long-term effectiveness is uncertain.

With this exposition complete, the movie proceeds to chronicle the next forty-eight hours of Catherine's life, during which the psychiatrist observes her behavior and attempts to awaken her memory of the traumatic event that underlies her illness. As one would expect of a Tennessee Williams play, it is no ordinary story, but a tale with symbolic dimensions of a parasitic mother–son relationship, repressed homosexuality, and, in its horrific conclusion, cannibalism.

When Dr. Cukrowicz and viewers meet Catherine, she is confined at St. Mary's, a Catholic "custodial home for the insane." She has been isolated as violent and, when outside her cell, she is carefully guarded. A few minutes of conversation with the psychiatrist, however, reveal her to be not only intelligent, sensitive, and kind-hearted but also aware of her predicament. She knows she is regarded as insane, but she is convinced she is sane and she is extremely frustrated that she has no memory of the reality which torments her.

Catherine is transferred to Lions View, but Dr. Cukrowicz takes an unorthodox approach by giving her a freedom other patients do not have. She is allowed to dress in street clothes, her room is in the nurses' section, and she can move about unsupervised. These liberties can be understood from a clinical perspective since the doctor is trying to assess the patient in an extraordinarily brief time, but they also occasion a couple of scenes that sensationalize mental illness. One of these scenes follows a visit by Catherine's mother and brother. Nearly hysterical after learning that her mother plans to sign commitment papers and a consent to operate, in return for a sizable inheritance from Aunt Violet, Catherine runs from her room and wanders onto a walkway within a men's ward. Soon male patients are clutching through the railing at her legs, and her hysteria turns to chilling screams. Later, Catherine wanders onto another walkway, this time within a women's ward, with the intent to jump over the railing. As she is rescued by a young, blond doctor, the women in the ward watch from below, some laughing, others crying and pacing.

Such moments seem designed to titillate the audience and exploit the public's fascination with asylums. Another distraction is the romantic license the story takes with the doctor–patient relationship. The first time Catherine kisses Dr. Cukrowicz, she realizes she should not have done so, but he asks, "Why not?" and says it was a friendly kiss. The second time she kisses him, she kisses him passionately, and neither he nor the hospital's director, who interrupts them, even comments on her behavior, although the director does look disapprovingly at them. At the end of the movie, after Catherine's dramatic recollection of Sebastian's death, she and the doctor walk off together, hand in hand, as the music swells. This romanticizing of the psychiatrist and the doctor–patient relationship weakens the credibility of the film, but it does not negate the film's sensitivity toward mental illness.

Nor does it weaken the thematic complexity of the film. Sebastian and Violet have tried to transcend the human condition by setting themselves above it, by, in fact, denying its reality. Unable to accept the flawed condition of humanity, Sebastian seeks a "purity" in art, culture, and people that is defined by his personal, elitist standards. Unable to live in a fallen Eden where both nature and God exert negative, even "devouring," force, he creates his own paradise, a garden of exotic vegetation that he has collected from his travels around the world. The garden at the Venable home, however, is no less corrupt than the world Sebastian and Violet reject. Dominated by insectivorous plants and adorned with winged skeletons, the garden threatens to devour.

Like the garden, Sebastian and his mother feed on others—young men and women, who hunger for wealth and society; Catherine, who hungers for friendship and hope; and, tragically, the children of a backward Mediterranean village, who hunger for both physical and spiritual nourishment. Catherine suddenly, temporarily, lost her memory last summer, but cousin Sebastian lost his humanity long before that. His madness, like Violet's at the film's end, might indeed be called hopeless.

Like the protagonists in the films discussed so far, the central character in Hall Bartlett's *The Caretakers* (1963) denies reality and suffers the consequences. Like *The Snake Pit* and *The Three Faces of Eve*, in plot and theme *The Caretakers* is concerned foremost with portraying mental illness and its treatment.

Probably relatively unknown, *The Caretakers* must be considered a breakthrough film on the subject of mental illness. The black-and-white photography, music, and title drawings combine to suggest that the movie is a state-of-the-art report on the mental health movement. The opening credits are superimposed on stills—paintings—of stylized and suffering human figures. Expressionistic in form, the stills recall paintings such as Edvard Munch's *The Scream*. Accompanying the images is a flamboyant musical score by Elmer Bernstein, the composer who also wrote scores for *To Kill a Mockingbird* and many other films. Throughout the movie the music of the opening credits functions as a theme song for the caretakers, the doctors and nurses who, like big-city cops, are working to eliminate mental illness from modern society.

Produced fifteen years after *The Snake Pit*, *The Caretakers* has many parallels with the earlier movie. First, its primary focus is the experience of one patient, Lorna Melford, played well by Polly Bergen, and her point of view helps make the mental patient's confusion and suffering real to viewers. Second, the film is concerned with the complexity of treating mental illness, especially as new psychiatric approaches emerge. Finally, its purposes are dual: to educate as well as to entertain.

The movie opens with a tracking shot of Lorna as she hurries along a busy city street, clutching her purse to her chest. She stops outside a movie theater and buys a ticket—the year is 1961, and *West Side Story*, billed as the best movie of the year, is playing. Certain sounds are exaggerated and painful to her; she holds her ears as the cash register rings. Inside the theater the sounds of the newsreel—rockets blasting off—increase her discomfort; close-ups show the agony in her face. Finally, she bolts from her seat and runs screaming to the stage. As she cries for help and attendants try to lead her away, she bats her arms at them in fear.

At Canterbury State Hospital, where Lorna's husband has had her admitted because they cannot afford a private hospital, viewers continue to experience Lorna's perspective. As she is wheeled down the halls on a gurney, viewers see the distorted images she sees: the blurred faces of hospital workers, the word *insane* being stamped over and over on the commitment order, and the giant keyhole of a locked door. Like Lewis Carroll's Alice, Lorna has fallen down a rabbit hole, and little here resembles ordinary reality. Like Virginia in *The Snake Pit*, she sees the grating on the windows and thinks she is in prison, believing that she has done something horrible and is being punished.

When Dr. Donovan MacLeod (Robert Stack) enters the story, the focus shifts to the role of the caretakers. Because Lorna has already been labeled as violent, she has been secluded, strapped to her bed, and placed in wrist and leg restraints. Dr. MacLeod disagrees with this traditional approach, and in his first interview with her he removes the restraints, talks with her, and manages to obtain a modicum of trust from her. He tells her that she will be transferred to "borderline," a women's ward which, under his supervision, uses new and experimental techniques in the treatment of patients. For one thing, the patients have the freedom to move about that they would have if they were in a community-based facility; and for another, the primary treatment is group therapy, which was just coming into vogue in the late 1950s and early 1960s.

The movie is sensitive to the complexity of mental illness and its treatment. The borderline patients represent a variety of conditions. Irene, an elderly woman, seems to suffer from chronic depression; Connie, who is in her late teens or early twenties, demonstrates classic symptoms of schizophrenia, including hallucinations and hearing voices; Edna is nearly catatonic and has not spoken in seven years; and Marion, Ana, and Lorna all seem to suffer the anxiety and depression that accompany traumatic childhoods or other traumatic experiences. In many cases there is no single cause. As Lorna's husband (Robert Vaughn) explains, Lorna's condition worsened after the death of their young son, but she has always been "a little different," lost in her own world and thoughts.

The complexity of treating mental illness is compounded by the changes and advances in the field. A parallel story line is the battle between Dr. MacLeod and the head nurse, Lucretia Terry, played venomously by Joan Crawford. Nurse Terry and her staff of senior nurses subscribe to the traditional techniques of caring for the mentally ill: isolating them from the healthy population and, in the case of aggressive or violent patients, restraining them, treating them with generous doses of electroconvulsive therapy, or otherwise controlling them with force. Dr. MacLeod and the young nurses he has brought to the hospital to staff his ward believe in freedom, rather than restraint. In addition to group therapy as a treatment modality, MacLeod is involved in getting the first "day hospitals," or community-based facilities, started.

Lucretia believes that mental health workers are custodians of the ill, whereas Dr. MacLeod believes the doctors and nurses are caretakers of "their hope" and "their future" while they are recuperating from illness. Lucretia is determined to sabotage the doctor's program, but the climactic final sequence of the film shows his methods to be not only effective but also important in the future of psychiatry. Patients Lorna, Marion, and Edna confront one another, and, in the process, each of them faces something painful but also liberating about herself. Even Nurse Bracken (Constance Ford), Lucretia's coconspirator, is stunned by the progress the patients make in this final group therapy session.

The conflicts among the staff are entertaining, but they also are instructive. When Dr. MacLeod addresses the new psychiatric nurses after they have witnessed group therapy on closed-circuit television, he is also lecturing the movie audience. One of every ten people is affected by mental illness, and mental illness takes up more hospital beds than all other diseases, he tells them. Most of these patients, however, are basically normal people who are mentally ill. Later, he asks Lorna's husband to remember a time when alcoholics were stigmatized, just as the mentally ill are today. In a touching scene the doctor holds up a box that his father once used to store his tobacco. The box is chipped and scarred; there are no perfect boxes, Dr. MacLeod explains, nor are there perfect people.

The *Caretakers* is an excellent film that opens viewers' eyes to the ordinariness of mental illness. The patients in the borderline ward include average American women whose situations are familiar to viewers: the young wife who cannot cope with knowing she will never have another child, or the woman who alternates between anger and depression because she was never loved as a child. The film would be a masterpiece had it remained focused on the patients and their situations. Unfortunately, many of these characters are undeveloped, and questions are left unanswered. Connie, for example, mentions her husband Freddie several times and he appears in one scene, but viewers never learn why he is introduced into the story. A more serious flaw in the movie is the introduction of extraneous story lines, such as romances that develop between some of the doctors and nurses.

Like several other films that cover the subject of mental illness, *The Caretakers* also succumbs to the temptation to shock viewers. ECT, which had been handled effectively in earlier films (*The Snake Pit; Fear Strikes Out*) is exploited in *The Caretakers*. Lorna receives only one ECT treatment, but it is photographed from start to finish. As the ECT violates her body, so does the camera, showing every twitch and spasm of her face, torso, and limbs. Later, the movie again sensationalizes its subject when Lorna becomes upset and runs away from a group gathering. In an interminably long sequence she runs down halls, hides until dark, and eventually ends up in a men's ward. As several men back her against a wall, the music reaches a fever pitch, her dress is torn, she screams, and the camera cuts to another scene of Lorna being packed with ice, having inexplicably been rescued from this lions' den. Clearly the story does not present the male patients with the dignity and respect Dr. MacLeod has urged for all the mentally ill.

The Caretakers is a flawed but nonetheless inspiring film. Robert Stack, Polly Bergen, Barbara Barrie (as Edna), and Janis Paige (as Marion) exhibit moments of brilliance that humanize mental illness and help to shatter the stigma so often associated with it. The movie ends with a still of Dr. MacLeod and these words superimposed on his image: "We are the caretakers of their hope—their future." This final shot punctuates what the movie has advocated, compassionate but professional care of mental illness.

The need to deny reality continues to figure prominently in movies of the 1960s and later movies that depict mentally ill characters. One very popular film was *Splendor in the Grass* (1961), produced and directed by Elia Kazan and written by William Inge, the Pulitzer Prize–winning author of *Picnic* and other plays. In this movie about young love, the heroine suffers a mental breakdown when she is unable to accept the loss of love.

The title of *Splendor in the Grass* comes from a poem by the nineteenth-century British poet William Wordsworth. In the poem, "Ode: Intimations of Immortality from Recollections of Early Childhood," Wordsworth contemplates the transition people make from youth, a state of innocence and idealism, to adulthood, a state informed by experience and disappointment. In the movie Miss Metcalf, the high school senior class English teacher, quotes from the poem:

What though the radiance which was once so bright
Is now for ever taken from my sight,
    Though nothing can bring back the hour
Of splendor in the grass, of glory in the flower;
    We will grieve not, rather find
Strength in what remains behind.

She asks Wilma Dean Loomis—Deanie, the film's heroine (Natalie Wood)—what the poet meant by these lines.

The moment is a painful one for Deanie. Her boyfriend, Bud Stamper (Warren Beatty in his film debut), has recently broken off their relationship and Deanie hears whispers that he is seeing Juanita, a classmate who has a reputation for not being "nice." In class Deanie says she did not hear the question, and so Miss Metcalf tells her to stand, recite the lines, and explain them. Deanie reads from the poem and offers an interpretation, as Juanita smiles up at her. Deanie breaks off in the middle of a sentence, walks tremblingly to the front of the room, asks to be excused, and then races from the classroom.

Like the speaker in Wordsworth's poem, Deanie is learning something about the world of experience. She and Bud deeply love each other, but they do not know how to deal with their emotions and desires. Set in Kansas in the late 1920s, the film pits the young lovers against Victorian attitudes about sexuality and passion. Seeking counsel from their parents leads to greater confusion. When Deanie asks her mother whether she ever felt for Mr. Loomis the feelings Deanie has for Bud, her mother responds that no nice girl has such feelings. Whenever the subject of Deanie and Bud's relationship arises, Mrs. Loomis is primarily concerned with whether they have gone "too far." When Bud tries to discuss his feelings with his father, old blowhard Ace Stamper (Pat Hingle) advises him that there are two kinds of girls: the nice kind like Deanie whom boys like Bud eventually marry and the not-so-respectable kind who can help Bud deal with his frustration.

For both Deanie and Bud the ideals of love and romance are being threatened by lies and hypocrisy. Deanie cannot cope with this clash of innocence and experience, youth and adulthood. Her response is not unlike that of Thel in "The Book of Thel," a poem by William Blake, another late-eighteenth and early-nineteenth-century writer who was concerned almost exclusively with these two contrary states. When the virgin Thel sees the "land of sorrows [and] of tears where never smile was seen," when she gains knowledge of death and the other realities of experience, "with a shriek" she "[flees] back" to the blissful valley of innocence (68). Deanie, too, runs with a shriek from this world of double standards that make love a dirty thing. She seeks her escape by attempting suicide at the falls outside of town. Young lovers in parked cars are roused by the cries of rescuers and her screams to be left alone.

Being told by the local doctor that their daughter is "in a very nervous condition," Mr. Loomis agrees to have Deanie transferred to a private mental hospital in Wichita. He had earlier considered getting help for his daughter, but his wife resisted, sure that there was nothing wrong with their daughter and noting, besides, that there have never been mental problems in the family. Certainly Deanie has given warning of her inability to cope; when Bud stopped seeing her she withdrew from friends, lost her appetite, even told her mother, "I want to die." When her mother suggested calling Bud, Deanie became nearly hysterical with fear that she should be so humiliated.

Deanie is subsequently hospitalized for two and a half years in Wichita. This stay seems inordinately long. Although Deanie and Bud were overly dependent on one another for emotional support, the film does not present enough evidence to warrant such an extended hospitalization. In fact, six months into her recuperation, she is already forming a romantic friendship with another patient, John, a young medical doctor who is hospitalized because he was unable to live up to his father's expectations that he continue his studies and become a surgeon. At the end of the film, Deanie is to be married to John.

Splendor in the Grass appealed to youth and romance devotees. It is not surprising that the treatment of Deanie's "nervous condition" is romanticized. The private hospital is a pleasant, gleaming white estate set on rolling hills—just the sort of idyllic setting where love might bloom again. Deanie's physician, Dr. Judd, is both wise and fatherly, not only listening patiently to her difficulties in relating to her parents but also taking an interest in her upcoming marriage to John and offering the advice that a loving parent might give.

When Deanie returns home, she tries to allay her mother's fears that the doctors in Wichita blamed Deanie's parents for her emotional problems. Earlier, at the hospital, Dr. Judd had cautioned Deanie that nowadays people want to blame their parents for their troubles. That perspective is enlightened, but, in fact, the movie has focused on the parents as the cause of the teenagers' confusion. When Deanie returns home, her mother continues her pattern of lies and evasions. Deanie will escape her mother's influence this time—because she is marrying John and moving to Cincinnati, not because she has demonstrated a newly acquired ability to stand alone.

Deanie has learned something about the transition from innocence to experience, however. At movie's end two old girlfriends drive her to Bud's ranch, and she visits with him, now married to Angelina, with one child and another on the way. Both Deanie and Bud seem happy with their new lives and admit that they no longer think too much about happiness. "You have to take what comes," Bud says. In the closing shot Deanie and her friends are driving away, and one of the friends asks, "Deanie, honey, do you still love him?" Deanie smiles and makes no reply, but in a voice-over she recites from Wordsworth's poem: "Though nothing can bring back the hour / Of splendor in the grass, of glory in the flower; / We will grieve not, rather find / Strength in what remains behind."

A more realistic portrayal of mental illness in adolescents is found in *David and Lisa* (1962), an independently made film directed by Frank Perry. Like *The Three Faces of Eve*, the script (by Eleanor Perry) is based on a similarly titled book written by a physician, Theodore Isaac Rubin, M.D. Set in a school for the emotionally disturbed, the story sensitively portrays seventeen-year-old David (Keir Dullea), who is withdrawn, antisocial, and refuses to be physically touched, and fifteen-year-old Lisa (Janet Margolin), who is schizophrenic and talks only in rhyme. The story traces David's progress under the care of Dr. Swinford (Howard da Silva) and the friendship that develops between David and Lisa.

The starkness of the characters' emotional lives is emphasized by the film's black-and-white photography. For David everything must be neatly, obsessively ordered. From his meticulous appearance to his insistence that clocks be accurate, he needs to feel he is in control of things. His refusal to let anyone touch him conceals a more profound refusal to feel anything emotionally toward others. When someone at the school forgets his rule and touches him, he agonizes that the person hates him and wants to kill him. Similarly, if he allows himself emotions, then he opens himself to another kind of hurt and pain. As David will not be touched, Lisa will not communicate. She rarely talks to the other students and teachers, and when she does speak, it is in very simple rhyme. She and David make a connection because he talks with her in rhyme and she agrees not to touch him.

Dr. Swinford tells David that Lisa has no choice about speaking in rhyme because she is sick. When people get well, the doctor says, then they are free to choose how they will behave. Lisa and David are both trapped by the limitations imposed by their illness. Repeatedly in the movie the characters are framed by windows and doors, or they are photographed against a background of windows and doors. At times the framing device helps to emphasize the idiosyncratic nature of their points of view. Although the doors and windows offer a variety of escapes, David and Lisa are trapped by their mental illnesses.

David and Lisa refuses to provide simple explanations and solutions. Viewers learn a little of David's home life and relationship with his parents, and nothing of Lisa's. Like *The Snake Pit*, the movie is not concerned with causes; instead, it concentrates on presenting the viewpoint of the person who is mentally ill. There are moments in the film when the camera gently leads viewers to sympathize with the characters. Just after David's arrival at the school, Dr. Swinford stops by his room to see if he is getting settled. David arrogantly rejects any overture on the doctor's part toward conversation or friendship. When Swinford leaves, the camera moves up and away, showing the boy sitting in a corner of the room, sobbing. On a field trip to an art museum in the city, Lisa is entranced by a large sculpture of a man and a woman with an infant on the woman's arm. She climbs upon the statue and nestles herself against the woman's breast. Just before she is forced to get down, there is a long shot from above. Both episodes capture not only the characters' inability to deal with their emotions but also their helplessness.

In another scene the film comments on the helplessness of the mentally ill, in general, to make their behavior socially acceptable. At the train station prior to the museum visit, Lisa approaches a waiting couple and their son; she is excited and happy by the signs of their Christmas shopping. When she speaks in rhyme, the boy wants to know what is wrong with her, and his father, speculating that she is from "that school," takes his family outside to wait for their train. As he stands in the doorway, he looks back at the group of students and yells, "Bunch of screwballs, spoiling the town." The camera moves outside the station, and the students follow. As they leave the building, one of them repeats the man's jeer, "Bunch of screwballs, spoiling the town." David repeats the words, and the chant continues with all the students joining in. As the family walks into the distance, appearing to be driven from the station, one of the teens begins to cry and even Carlos, tough and street smart, is tormented by the incident. With the close-up of the students' faces, however, their humanity triumphs over the stereotypes that sometimes blind other people.

The denial of reality figures strongly, too, in Robert Redford's *Ordinary People* (1980), an exceptionally well-acted and well-directed film that dramatizes the effect of mental illness on families. The story, adapted by Alvin Sargent from Judith Guest's novel, shows a family that is falling apart. Socioeconomically, these are not ordinary people; they are an upper-middle-class family living in the affluent Chicago suburb of Lake Forest. Calvin (Donald Sutherland) is a successful tax attorney, and Beth (Mary Tyler Moore) is a stay-at-home mom whose most difficult decisions revolve around scheduling her golf games and the couple's social obligations. At least they were not ordinary people until a few months before the story begins. It was then that their oldest son, Buck, died in a boating accident. The younger son, Conrad (Timothy Hutton) was with Buck at the time of the accident. As the film begins, the guilt-ridden Connie has been out of the hospital about a month, following four months of psychiatric treatment after a suicide attempt. The family is now trying to recover from its loss.

Life for this family, which once seemed perfect, has become, to use Calvin's word, something of a "mess." Beth wants them to get back to normal, but Calvin sees the difficulty his son is having in resuming his old life. Conrad eats and sleeps sporadically, is edgy and moody, and is trying to return, very shakily, to his old friendships and high school activities. His father is bewildered by his son's behavior and desperately wants to understand and help him. Beth, on the other hand, wants her and Calvin to get off by themselves for a while. Although she does not say so, she wants to get as far away from Conrad as she can.

The catalyst for resolving this mess is Conrad. His continuing illness pits his father squarely against his mother. When Conrad decides to continue therapy and makes an appointment with Dr. Berger, Calvin approves. He had earlier encouraged his son to continue treatment. Beth disapproves and is embarrassed; the stigma of mental illness makes her implacable. Family problems are private, she believes, and only weak people find themselves in her son's position. In one scene, Conrad accuses his mother of hating him, pointing out that she never even visited him in the hospital and she would have, had it been Buck. Buck, she throws in Conrad's face, would never have been in a hospital.

Ordinary People condemns prejudice against the mentally ill and shows it to be deeply ingrained. Beth's attitude is shared by her mother. They speak in embarrassed and judgmental tones about Conrad's visiting a psychiatrist; they are concerned about where Dr. Berger's office is located—are they relieved that it is in Highland Park, not Lake Forest? The stigma of mental illness is treated elsewhere in the film. A subplot shows how another adolescent is struggling with mental illness. When Conrad was in the hospital, he formed a friendship with Karen (Dinah Manoff). She, too, is trying to resume her life as a high school student. When she and Conrad meet for sodas one afternoon, viewers see that she is working hard at seeming well. When Conrad asks if she is still seeing a doctor, she tells him she is not—she agrees with her father that she is the only person who can help her. The event that precipitates the climax of the film is Connie's learning that Karen has committed suicide. Like Karen's father, Conrad's swimming coach is uninformed about mental illness. With unabashed curiosity, he wants to know about Connie's hospitalization and treatment. Not only does he want to know whether the athlete had shock therapy, but when Connie tells him yes, the coach gives the impression that his knowledge of such things is based in horror movies.

Dr. Berger (Judd Hirsch) knows both the stigma Connie must battle and the teen's inability to face his emotions. During the initial interview, the doctor asks him how he is feeling—depressed? as though he is on stage, that is, as though people regard him as a "dangerous character"? This eminently human psychiatrist—he wears a ratty sweater rather than the stereotypical blazer, and smokes cigarettes rather than a pipe—relies on honest and sometimes confrontational psychotherapy to help Conrad explore his guilt and his relationships with his family. When Connie is told on the telephone that Karen is dead, he panics. Not only has he lost a friend, but he feels overwhelming guilt and fear. It is late in the evening, but Dr. Berger agrees to meet him at the office. After months of talk that seems to Connie to go nowhere, he is finally made to face the reality of his pain. In this moment of crisis Berger questions, confronts, badgers his patient until Conrad finally articulates the guilt he feels, not only for having failed to save Buck from drowning but also for having survived an accident that his older, stronger brother could not survive.

Psychiatrist Irving Schneider criticizes the character of Dr. Berger as too good to be true, "what the public wants the good psychiatrist to be and, judging from the profession's response [to *Ordinary People*], what good psychiatrists want to be" (1002). Berger is accessible to his patient, talks and listens as though Conrad is his only patient, and seems indifferent to the outward trappings of a successful practice—plush office, prime location, and so forth. In these ways, the psychiatrist is an ideal parent, according to Schneider. The point is debatable. For all of his flexibility and attentiveness to the patient, Berger is willing to end a session after fifty minutes, even if ending it irritates or angers Conrad. Then, too, even as a well-decorated and furnished office may smack of professional success, the lived-in, somewhat shoddy environs of Dr. Berger's office does not initially inspire confidence, from Conrad or from viewers. Berger wins the trust of both the patient and the audience as the doctor–patient relationship develops.

When depicted effectively, mental illness has been, for the most part, restricted to serious drama. There are some noteworthy exceptions, however, in the comedy, romance, and suspense genres. One of the most effective comedy-romances to tackle the topic has been *As Good As It Gets* (1998), directed by James L. Brooks and cowritten by Brooks and Mark Andrus.

Early in this film, gay artist Simon Bishop (Greg Kinnear) explains his approach to his art. "I watch," he says. He watches until he finds a telling moment or expression, and then he paints. "You look at someone long enough," he says, "you discover their humanity." In the case of his neighbor, Melvin Udall (Jack Nicholson), Simon has to watch a long time because Udall has denied his own humanity and the worth of other people for a long time. Melvin is an obnoxious, at times reprehensible, misanthrope. He is homophobic and anti-Semitic, and Simon's black art dealer Frank (Cuba Gooding, Jr.) has no trouble making Melvin believe that he is, beneath the polish, a thug. Crudity and cruelty are Melvin's standard responses to people. At the restaurant where he routinely eats, a couple whom he assumes are Jewish must suffer his ethnic jokes. An overweight waitress who annoys him is addressed as "elephant girl." Even Carol, the good-hearted waitress, played lovingly by Helen Hunt, who patiently tolerates his behavior, has to endure a cruel comment about her chronically sick son.

Melvin, however, is not only obnoxious; he is also sick. Viewers even vaguely familiar with OCD—obsessive compulsive disorder—recognize the symptoms in Melvin early in the film. After being in public, which includes the hallway of his Manhattan apartment building, he repeatedly washes his hands in scalding water, each washing commencing with the opening of a fresh bar of soap. He locks, checks, and checks again that he has locked each of several bolts on his door. He tests light switches as he enters each room of his apartment by flipping them on and off five times. His apartment is in a state of meticulous order and cleanliness. When he does go out—he also is agoraphobic—he never steps on the cracks in the sidewalks, and he cautions, "Don't touch," when people approach.

Chanting his warning like a mantra, Melvin is a slave to ritual. When he awakens in the morning, he has the wherewithal to keep his feet from touching the floor because he has precisely positioned his slippers the night before for a safe landing. This slavishness to formula, however, has worked well in his professional life. He is a best-selling writer of more than sixty romance novels. Repetition of a formulaic plot and stereotypical heroines has made both him and his publisher a fortune.

Melvin's obsessions and compulsions are evident to anyone who sees something of his life and routine. The fact that his illness is so visible makes him vulnerable. As his friendship with Simon grows, Simon says, "One of the best things you have going for you is your ability to humiliate yourself." That vulnerability enables people like Simon and Carol to discover his humanity, and in the process they help him to face the realities of being human, with all its disorder and imperfections. Like a child learning table manners, Melvin learns not only how to dine but how to interact with people. As he does so, he begins, slowly indeed, to shed his old behavior. In the early restaurant scenes, Melvin insists on sitting at the same table every day and being served by Carol. He orders the same meal and eats it with his own plastic dinnerware. Later in the film he is seated with Carol in a swanky restaurant, not even in New York, but in Baltimore. Granted, he has yelled their order to a waiter across the room, and the dinner is aborted because Carol has walked out after being insulted, once again, by Melvin. Progress is being made, though.

As Good As It Gets gives a realistic and warm portrayal of mental illness. Melvin is seeing a psychiatrist for his condition, and, inspired by his feelings for Carol, he even begins to take the medication that has been prescribed. But recovery, in this case, behavior modification, is slow and not effortless. The point is made beautifully at the end. Out for an early morning walk, Carol and Melvin are about to enter a little bakery that has just opened. She has been walking on the bricked street, he on the sidewalk. As he holds the bakery door open for her, he inadvertently steps on the bricks. He looks down at—watches—his foot in pleasant amazement, perhaps at his own humanity.

CHAPTER THREE

~

Hitchcock, Chaos, and the Devils of Unreason

Dozens of movies have used madness to evoke horror and suspense. Most of these, including *What Ever Happened to Baby Jane?* (1962) and *Hush . . . Hush, Sweet Charlotte* (1964) from director Robert Aldrich, and Stanley Kubrick's box office success *The Shining* (1980), are worth only cursory attention for the serious viewer interested in gaining insights about cinema's depiction of mental illness. Alfred Hitchcock's fascination with the psyche and psychosis, however, resulted in a number of films that not only succeed as thrillers and mysteries but also thoughtfully portray mental illness, causing viewers to question and sometimes alter their perceptions about sanity, mental illness, and reality itself. Of the fifty-plus feature films he directed, many are in the suspense genre (Katz 634–635). They are tales of murder, blackmail, spies and counterspies, mistaken and assumed identities, sabotage, mysterious disappearances and kidnappings, assassination plots, and homicidal maniacs, including those of the feathered species. Amid the suspense and the action, these films have a surprisingly psychological dimension in plot, theme, and technique. The director is concerned with the characters' internal struggles, and in some films he turns the camera to a variety of mental conditions—amnesia, phobias, kleptomania, multiple personality. In the most effective of these films he uses these conditions as much more than plot devices. He uses them to explore characters' psychological conflicts and their efforts to deal with mental and emotional chaos.

The frequency with which mental illness occurs in Hitchcock's films is itself notable. In *Rebecca* (1940) one of the antagonists, Mrs. Danvers, is psychotic and delusional. In *Shadow of a Doubt* (1942) the chief antagonist, Uncle Charlie, is psychotic and homicidal, and his niece, in a doppelganger link, begins to exhibit signs of instability. In *Spellbound* (1945) the hero suffers from amnesia, triggered by memories of a traumatic childhood event. Additionally, the film's antagonist, Dr. Murchison, has experienced an emotional collapse prior to the action of the story. In *The Man Who Knew Too Much* (1955) the protagonist's wife has a history of emotional instability and requires medication. In *The Wrong Man* (1957) the hero's wife suffers a breakdown during the course of the story and remains hospitalized at the movie's end. In *Vertigo* (1958) the protagonist suffers from acrophobia and vertigo, and following the story's traumatic climax he is hospitalized in a psychiatric facility. In *Psycho* (1960) the now legendary Norman Bates (Anthony Perkins) suffers from the condition once known as multiple personality. In *The Birds* (1963) a secondary, but thematically significant, character has an almost pathological fear of being abandoned by her son. In *Marnie* (1964) the protagonist is a kleptomaniac and has a morbid fear of intimacy.

These characters are not ghouls and goblins. With the exception of Norman Bates, these characters rise above the stereotypes found in exploitative horror movies. Even though the story may seem outrageous—a slice of "cake," rather than a slice of "life," as Hitchcock described it (Truffaut 71)—the characters, for the most part, are ordinary people, living fairly ordinary lives. Mental illness in Hitchcock's films is, in fact, a part of everyday life. His stated objective was to produce "a completely unbelievable story told to the readers with such a spellbinding logic that you get the impression that the same thing could happen to you tomorrow" (qtd. in Perry).

The characters' internal struggles are common human dilemmas. In *Vertigo*, John "Scottie" Ferguson is a detective, a bachelor, and a man searching for an identity; his fears are manifested in acrophobia and vertigo. In *The Wrong Man* (1957), Manny and his wife, Rose, struggle with the day-to-day financial trials of raising a family; when crisis strikes, Rose can struggle no longer and suffers a nervous breakdown. In *Psycho*,

Norman's psyche has responded to the horrifying realities and losses of life by dissociating into two distinct identities. In *Marnie*, the title character struggles unconsciously with a childhood trauma she cannot remember by becoming a thief and pathological liar. Lesser characters suffer, too. In *Rebecca*, Mrs. Danvers cannot accept the death of Rebecca and descends into psychosis. In *Spellbound*, before the action of the film, Dr. Murchison had a nervous breakdown, which seems to have played a part in his losing his position at Green Manors hospital. In *Vertigo*, Judy Barton so desperately seeks love that she allows herself to be manipulated and changed in order to please her lovers, suggesting strongly that she suffers from borderline personality disorder.[3] In *The Birds*, Lydia Brenner is still mourning the death of her husband and has almost a pathological fear of being abandoned by her son.

Even the early *Rebecca* (1940) is as much a psychological drama as it is a suspense tale. A meek, plain American—a secretary and lady's companion (Joan Fontaine)—meets wealthy Britisher Maxim de Winter (Laurence Olivier) while she and her employer travel in Monte Carlo. After a whirlwind courtship, the protagonist, who remains unnamed as in Daphne du Maurier's novel of the same title, marries de Winter, whose first wife, Rebecca, died in a mysterious boating accident just one year before. At Manderley, de Winter's estate, the memory of Rebecca dominates, creating a suspense that is not resolved until an investigation of her death occurs in the last part of the film. The story is as much about "psychic horror" (Spoto 90), however, as it is about suspicious death. It is about the psychological power of guilt and jealousy, and the hold of the past on the mind, what Donald Spoto calls "the power of the dead to affect the living" (93) and notes in numerous Hitchcock films: *Spellbound* (1945), *Vertigo* (1958), *Psycho* (1960), *The Birds* (1963), and *Marnie* (1964).

Hitchcock called *Rebecca* an "old-fashioned" story, apparently because of its Gothic and romance elements (Truffaut 91–92). Some of the techniques, however, that give the movie the atmosphere of an Anne Radcliffe novel also emphasize the psychological drama of the characters. A contrast of light and shadows is one of these devices, and a movement from the exterior of buildings to the interior is another.[4] In the black-and-white *Rebecca* shadows are used superbly in a segment that occurs in the first weeks of the de Winters' return to Manderley. The protagonist is motivated when she sees a movement at a window in the west wing of the mansion to explore that part of the house, a forbidden area which houses Rebecca's old room and which has been closed off since her death. Rebecca's room is lit and photographed to suggest a sacred place, and Fontaine moves about surreptitiously. Suddenly she is startled by the appearance of Mrs. Danvers (Judith Anderson), the ominous housekeeper who is obsessively devoted to the memory of her former employer. Mrs. Danvers appears as a larger-than-life shadow hovering over the timid and unworldly protagonist. Hitchcock's use of shadows in the segment, however, does more than create Gothic suspense. The shadowed figure of Mrs. Danvers also serves as an eerie reminder of Rebecca's presence and power over Fontaine, and it emphasizes Fontaine's sense of inadequacy as the new Mrs. de Winter.

In her aloof manner, severe appearance, and mechanical movements Mrs. Danvers is nearly one-dimensional. Haunted by memories of Rebecca, she is completely distanced from the present. Psychotic and delusional, she eventually sets fire to Manderley and perishes in the blaze. Her dark presence suggests an evil force and inspires terror in the heroine. By story's end, however, those distinctions belong to Rebecca, who deceived and manipulated "Danny," her most loyal fan, as unfeelingly as she deceived her husband and all of her other unsuspecting victims.

The most conspicuously psychological of Hitchcock's early movies is *Spellbound*, produced in 1945 by David O. Selznick. The credits even list May E. Romm, M.D., as the film's psychiatric advisor. *Spellbound* is ostensibly concerned with dramatizing how psychoanalysis works. Following the opening credits, a line from Shakespeare appears on the screen: "The fault . . . is not in our stars, but in ourselves." The line is from the tragedy *Julius Caesar*, where Cassius is telling fellow conspirator Brutus that humans indeed have control of their fates. How humans manage that is explained in a second quote:

> Our story deals with psychoanalysis, the method by which modern science treats the emotional problems of the sane. The analyst seeks only to induce the patient to talk about his hidden problems, to open the locked doors of his mind.
>
> Once the complexes that have been disturbing the patient are uncovered and interpreted, the illness and confusion disappear . . . and the devils of unreason are driven from the human soul.

The words read like the book jacket of a late-twentieth-century self-improvement text. "Having trouble with the boss's management style, feeling envious of his power and prestige?" the book teases. Here is help, a medically proven technique for dealing with resentment and guilt.

As with other Hitchcock films, however, it is not that simple. In *Spellbound* there is genuine enthusiasm for psychoanalysis; the very resolution of the plot evolves from the psychoanalyst's ability to solve the riddle presented by the patient's dream. The complexity lies in the difficulty of distinguishing the dream from the reality, of categorizing reason from unreason, and of recognizing the sane from the insane. As will also be seen in *Psycho* and *Vertigo*, what appears to be so is not necessarily the reality.[5]

In the opening of the story, the staff of a psychiatric hospital, Green Manors, is awaiting the arrival of Dr. Anthony Edwardes, who is to replace Dr. Murchison (Leo G. Carroll) as head of the facility. Murchison has been fired by the Board following an illness brought on by overwork and mental fatigue. Edwardes (Gregory Peck) arrives but quickly displays signs of mental disturbance. A promising young psychiatrist on the staff, Dr. Constance Peterson (Ingrid Bergman), is intrigued by his behavior and manages to discover not only that he is not Edwardes but that he is suffering from amnesia and believes he killed Edwardes. Driven by professional interest as well as an emotional and romantic attraction to him, she takes on the task of curing him.

That Edwardes is not who he initially seems to be is only the first of several deceiving appearances in *Spellbound*. Dr. Murchison, who seems to be fully recovered from his nervous collapse and resigned to relinquish Green Manors to a successor, is far from well. Dr. Peterson, who seems firmly governed by reason—is even accused of being without emotion by an amorous colleague—is strongly motivated by her passion for the patient. When he flees Green Manors, Edwardes, now identified by the police as an impostor, is described over radio broadcasts as a "dangerous madman." On the contrary, as a result of the trauma he has experienced but cannot remember, he vacillates between a state of near catatonia and suicide. Never does he appear to be a danger to anyone else.

The movie is populated by impostors. Murchison is not a well-balanced, rational administrator but a murderer. Edwardes is not Edwardes but John Ballantine, and John Ballantine is not a murderer but an unwitting witness to murder. Even some of the patients at Green Manors are impostors: Mary Carmichael purports to be a nymphomaniac but actually fears and loathes men, and a male patient, Garmes, mistakenly believes himself to be guilty of patricide. The impostor motif figures elsewhere, too. Constance Peterson twice pretends to be someone she is not. In a hotel lobby in New York City, she poses as the wife of John Brown, actually John Ballantine, to get information from the house detective. Even the detective admits to wearing a mask occasionally, that of would-be psychologist and reader of human nature. Later, Peterson and Ballantine pose as newlyweds when they seek refuge in the home of her former teacher, an aging but capable psychiatrist (Michael Chekhov).

John Ballantine is visibly spellbound—signaled by the trancelike stare and demeanor that come over him as memories burst into his consciousness. Quite a few of the other characters also are under a spell. Like Ballantine, the patient Garmes is guilt-ridden in the extreme. Like Murchison, the patient Carmichael is bedeviled by fear and hatred. Constance Peterson, of course, behaves at times as though love-struck. To what extent, then, are these characters in control of their fates? On one hand, the film confidently parades psychoanalysis and psychiatry as the tools by which people can explore their problems and understand the forces that motivate them. On the other hand, the film confronts viewers with the paradox that Freud, Jung, and the whole of psychoanalysis articulated: namely, that these hitherto unknown forces exist and are buried in the subconscious. Modern science can be cold comfort to the person who has no or little awareness, and even less control, of his fear, guilt, or envy. In his frustration to discover his identity, *Spellbound*'s John Ballantine calls Freud "hooey."

The paradox is beautifully visualized in Ballantine's dream and in several dreamlike episodes in the movie. The dream sequence is based on designs created by Salvador Dali and, like the paintings of the great surrealist, it blends photographic realism with the incongruities of the dream state. As the sequence begins, giant eyes appear to swim on the screen but emerge as part of window drapes that someone is cutting with larger-than-life scissors. Characters in the dream, depicted as Ballantine recounts it for the psychiatrists, seem real enough but float against an undulating, changing backdrop. Toward the end of the dream, the shadow of a huge winged creature dominates the screen, hovering over the patient, he says. The use of black-and-white film, rather than diminishing the realism of the images, emphasizes the contrast and the conflict of dream and reality. It is the conflict that tortures the patient. Before knowing for certain, John Ballantine senses some of the truth of his experience: for example, that Edwardes is dead. Throughout the story, however, he cannot be sure of what is real and what is imagined, what is memory and what is simply inexplicable.

This surrealistic effect is again achieved in the sequence immediately following the dream narrative. Ballantine says, "Something's happening," knowing without looking that snow has begun to fall. The moment is important because the snow and images resembling ski tracks stir memories of the trauma his conscious mind has erased. Just as Hitchcock's Marnie in the movie of that title becomes nearly hysterical every time she sees red, Ballantine becomes agitated when he sees the color white. Constance drawing a pattern with her fork on a white tablecloth, her white bath robe patterned with dark ridges, the hospital surgery with its predominance of white gowns and bright lights, a white bed cover with raised vertical lines, the bathroom at the old psychiatrist's home with its white porcelain and furnishings: all these images drive him to the edge of remembering.

With Ballantine's announcement, the doctors—and the camera—turn to face and then look out the window of the study. Looking through the window onto the street and falling snow is like gazing into one of those watery snow globes containing a village scene. The details of the street, sled tracks, and houses seem solid and distinct, but they become indistinct in the swirling snow. The image is a metaphor for Ballantine's mental state, as memory begins to emerge but then recedes, locked in his state of forgetfulness.

From the refuge of the old psychiatrist's home, Ballantine and Peterson travel to Gabriel Valley, a ski lodge they have identified from the dream as the place where Edwardes met his death in what she presumes to be a skiing accident. In an effort to reenact the event, they ski down the mountain, and the sequence ends with Ballantine remembering a childhood trauma, just in the nick of time, so to speak, as he stops them from going over a precipice. The root of his guilt complex, it turns out, was the accidental death of his brother, which he witnessed and for which he has always blamed himself. Like Virginia in *The Snake Pit*, Conrad in *Ordinary People*, and other movie characters, he has not consciously confronted the past event. Witnessing the death of Edwardes, Dr. Peterson explains, triggered his deeply rooted feelings of guilt. The ski tracks parallel the earlier image of his young brother being accidentally impaled on the spiked iron bars of a yard fence.

As in some sequences of *Marnie*, Hitchcock used rear projections to film the ski sequence. Location shooting might have made the sequence more realistic. Yet, it is the surrealistic effect of the characters existing and moving as though separate from the setting that makes this sequence effective and contributes to the unity of the film. Is the event, the film asks, real or part of Ballantine's dream?

Nor is the confusion of dream versus reality cleared up when the patient remembers witnessing Dr. Edwardes falling over the precipice. Shortly after, when Ballantine is arrested for the murder of Edwardes—a bullet has been found in the body—Hitchcock continues the surrealistic blending of images. The story seems to fast forward, showing Ballantine being convicted and then imprisoned; and the images of Constance Peterson testifying in court and prison doors being opened and shut are shot against a backdrop of clouds. The prison bars juxtaposed against the white echoes the earlier images that have haunted the patient.

John Ballantine's predicament in *Spellbound*, his inability to trust his memory as reality, is not a condition experienced only by the patient. Psychiatry, like all science, depends on what can be verified and what can be observed. To Constance's old mentor, who has a disheveled and slightly comic resemblance to Freud himself, the patient presents the outward signs of a person who is schizophrenic and quite possibly homicidal. When the doctor wants to call the police, she talks him out of it. "The mind isn't everything," she says. There is the truth of what her heart tells her. He gives in, reluctantly, to her pleadings that the patient is not dangerous: "You are twenty times crazier than he is," her friend chides.

In the end, science is wrong, and Peterson's intuition and passion are correct. It was Dr. Murchison who murdered Edwardes. Back at Green Manors, Peterson confronts Murchison with the last pieces of the dream's puzzle, which identifies Murchison as the murderer. Cornered, he pulls from his desk the revolver he used to kill Edwardes and points it at his colleague. Rather than be convicted and imprisoned or executed, however, he slowly turns the gun toward himself, and the camera records this action from his point of view, so that the audience is staring down the barrel of the gun. When he shoots, the screen is suffused with red, the only time Hitchcock uses color in the film. The red of Murchison's passion gone awry finally obliterates the images of white that have dominated. The images of snow and tracks in the snow were the evidence that the doctors and movie viewers used to try to discover Ballantine's identity. The puzzle is pieced together, however, only with the aid of Constance's constancy, her passionate belief in her feelings toward John Ballantine.

Science is limited in its ability to distinguish the dream from the reality. Nor are perception, logic, and reason totally reliable tools to diagnose the insane from the sane. *Spellbound* remains a classic, in part, because it expresses this age-old struggle of reason and imagination. The winged creature hovering over John Ballantine in his dream seems at first to Constance to be a witch or harpy. Her former teacher interprets it as an angel, as it indeed is in the language of dreams: a code image for Gabriel Valley. He also sees the angelic figure as a symbol for Constance, since she is the one aspiring to save Ballantine, who sees himself as a devilish murderer. She is the light of reason that will rescue him from the "devils of unreason." She succeeds in rescuing him, however, because she affirms both science and intuition and coaxes them to work collaboratively.

The "devils of unreason" that preoccupy *Spellbound* recur in other films. In creating characters who, like Ballantine, are mentally ill, Hitchcock depicts them realistically and compassionately. Part of the chill that goes up viewers' spines the first time they see *Psycho* derives from the sympathy they feel for Norman Bates and perhaps even a slight identification with him. He says to Marion Crane, "we all go a little mad from time to time." She responds, "Sometimes just one time can be enough," implying that she has gone mad at least once. The larger implication is that it can happen to anyone. Like ancient Greek theatergoers, viewers feel both fear and pity. They pity Norman, but they also fear for themselves because of what fate or the world can impose on them. Like Norman, perhaps anyone can be driven to madness. Certainly, as millions experience each year, anyone can succumb to mental illness.

This possibility is treated chillingly in *Shadow of a Doubt*. The film's antagonist is psychopathic, but the film suggests that someone as ordinary and innocent as the film's heroine can go mad as well. The story concerns the friendship of a young woman, Charlotte/"Charlie" (Teresa Wright) with her Uncle Charlie (Joseph Cotton), for whom she is named. He has come, unexpectedly, from Philadelphia to visit his sister's family in the sleepy little town of Santa Rosa, California. His arrival is an answer to Charlie's prayer that something happen to interrupt the boring routine of her and her family's lives. What Charlie does not know about her uncle is that he is running from the law, suspected of murdering several wealthy widows in various East Coast cities.

This niece and her uncle share more than their name. From the start, the two characters are shown to mirror each other. The opening sequences establish the parallel. The film opens with an aerial view of a large city, and in characteristic Hitchcock fashion the camera tracks from the city to a neighborhood of brick tenements to, and through, the window of a boardinghouse to a particular room, where Joseph Cotton is sprawled languidly on his back on the bed. His landlady stops by to tell him of two gentlemen who have been looking for him. She remarks that he looks tired. The cash strewn on the floor by his bed suggests more than physical exhaustion, perhaps a weariness with the world and his life. Shortly after, he leaves the boardinghouse, followed by the two fellows who have been waiting on the street corner. The sequence ends as he manages to give them the slip. The camera cuts to a parallel shot of Santa Rosa and tracks to an inviting house in a residential neighborhood and finally to young Charlie lying on a bed, her legs crossed at the ankles in a pose similar to Uncle Charlie's earlier. When her father comes into her room and asks if she is sick, she describes ennui that echoes Uncle Charlie's apparent world weariness.

The mirror images highlight a striking similarity in the characters. Both the niece and the uncle are alone and unattached. Uncle Charlie's lifestyle emphasizes his isolation: his home is a room in a boardinghouse and his "business"—never clearly spelled out, for obvious reasons—takes him from city to city. Although niece Charlie lives with her family, it has been several years since her high school graduation and it is not clear whether she works. Nor does she seem to have any romantic prospects. There is something private, secret, about each of them, young Charlie explains to her uncle. They don't tell people many things about themselves. Outwardly they pride themselves on their independent thinking, and they long to be more than average. The niece is captivated by the uncle's Byronic nonconformity. Emotionally, however, each is childish and childlike. She avoids growing up by remaining at home, grousing about the ordinariness of her life while hoping for something magical to happen to transform her life. The uncle returns home to his sister—surrogate mother—when his perverse child's play catches up with him.

The screen is occasionally filled with the image of couples dancing to the tune of the Merry Widow waltz, swirling like riders on a carousel. The air of magic initially suggested by the image dissipates as it is repeated, following each new revelation about the identity of Uncle Charlie. Coincidentally, when he first arrives in Santa Rosa, his niece inexplicably hums the tune, at first not being able to identify it and then hating it when she learns its name and learns from detectives that the killer they seek has been dubbed the Merry Widow murderer.

As Charlie learns the truth about her uncle, she, too, changes. She begins to behave erratically, in some ways resembling her uncle. On his first day in Santa Rosa, she runs around the house, her mother happily declares, "like she's lost her mind." As his visit continues, however, her behavior is more disturbing. Unknowingly, she is drawn into his deceit. When he tears up her father's newspaper (to remove an article about the search for the murderer), she instinctively refolds it carefully with the hope that "Pop won't notice." As her suspicions about her uncle grow and are confirmed by newspaper clippings and the detectives who are tracking him, she becomes physically and emotionally exhausted, snapping at her family and sleeping late like Uncle Charlie. As she races about Santa Rosa, she arouses the concern of people who have known her since infancy. In the film's conclusion, she is most dramatically linked to her uncle. At his coaxing she boards the train as he prepares to leave Santa Rosa. As he tries to push her from the moving train, to silence the only person who knows his guilt, she fights him off, accidentally causing him to fall onto the tracks in front of an oncoming train. Like him, she has killed.

At first glance *Shadow of a Doubt* suggests that Uncle Charlie is simply evil. He certainly talks like a person who does not believe in the existence of good. The world is a joke, he tells his niece, and most people live like swine. The story indicates, however, that mental illness may be the cause of his behavior, stemming from a skull fracture he suffered as a child. The injury left him agitated and hyperactive.

The chaos that Uncle Charlie's childhood accident introduced is part of a larger theme of chaos in the movie.[6] Chaos enters characters' lives, disconnecting them from their past and the forces of order and reason. Uncle Charlie frequently laments the state of the current world and longs for a past when life was sweeter. The life he lives brings him no pleasure, and he is tired of running from the police. The chaos he brings into his niece's life results in her loss of innocence, a firsthand encounter with the unpredictable, destructive forces in the world. In the final scene she tells her newfound friend and love interest (Macdonald Carey), one of the detectives who has pursued the case, that Uncle Charlie believed the world is a sordid place. She asks Jack if he agrees. He doesn't agree, he says, but "sometimes it [the world] needs a lot of watching. It seems to go crazy every now and then, like your Uncle Charlie."

In other Hitchcock films there is a similar emphasis on chaos as an inescapable part of life. Furthermore, "craziness," or mental illness, is simply a manifestation of the chaos. In *The Wrong Man* chaos enters the lives of the protagonist and his wife when he is mistakenly identified and accused as a holdup man. The chaos is internalized when she has a mental collapse and must be hospitalized. In *The Man Who Knew Too Much* the protagonist and his wife are swept into a sea of chaos when he inadvertently learns about an assassination plot. Again, one of the manifestations of the chaos is her emotional instability in responding to the ensuing crisis. In *The Birds* chaos comes in the form of attacking birds. The ordeal leaves the heroine in a state of shock and confusion.

Nor does chaos always have a clear cause in Hitchcock's films. Certainly in some of these movies, such as *Rebecca*, *Spellbound*, and *Marnie*, the chaos and "craziness" have identifiable causes. In some others, however, the chaos seems random, as suggested by Norman Bates's words: "We all go a little mad from time to time." In *The Man Who Knew Too Much*, Jo McKenna (Doris Day) longs to know why she and her family were chosen by the conspirators, but in the end she must be content with the words she sings several times: "Que sera, sera" ("What will be, will be"). In *The Birds* the characters attempt to find an explanation for the bird attacks on the people of Bodega Bay. The way the birds mass and then attack "seems like a pattern," but the townspeople cannot uncover any clear cause–effect relationship. The world, Hitchcock's films say, is too complex and dynamic for such linear explanations.

In many of the films, however, there is a recurring pattern in the chaos the characters experience. Often the central characters are initially restless, discontent, or frustrated with the stasis of their lives (Spoto 268, 270, 304, 306, 388). In *Rebecca* the life of the protagonist is the tedious, uninterrupted routine of a woman's companion. In *Shadow of a Doubt* young Charlie is unhappy that her family is in "a rut"—nothing is happening, she laments. In *The Wrong Man*, Manny's wife, Rose (Vera Miles), is discontented with their financial situation—they seem to just get the bills and loans paid and then are forced to go back into debt. In *Vertigo*, Scottie has been dominated by restlessness—first he attended law school, then joined the police force; he was engaged, then was rejected. In *The Man Who Knew Too Much*, the McKennas are on an extended vacation, possibly coping with discontent in their marriage. In *The Birds*, Melanie is growing weary of her playgirl lifestyle and its emptiness. In *Psycho*, Marion is tired of the sordidness of her relationship with Sam. In *Marnie* the heroine's life is a relentless cycle of criminal activity.

Into each of these lives comes the unpredictable, a chaos the characters had not bargained on. Their response to the chaos is part of their journey. As they travel through Hitchcock's recurring motifs of stairs and corridors, churches and bell towers, hotel and hospital rooms, winding roads and traffic, they endure the chaos and even sometimes triumph.

In *Vertigo* (1958), probably Hitchcock's most famous film, the restless, somewhat aimless life of John "Scottie" Ferguson (James Stewart) is thrown into chaos by a mental condition, the phobia known as fear of heights, that incapacitates him. The opening sequences introduce the protagonist and his predicament. A young male is being chased on building rooftops by a uniformed policeman, followed by the James Stewart character. Stewart slips, slides down a roof, and hangs perilously from loosened guttering. As the character looks down to the street, he is overcome by vertigo and unable to respond to the cop's urge to grab his hand. The cop himself then slips and falls to his death. The film cuts to a scene in the apartment of Stewart's friend, Midge (Barbara Bel Geddes). Detective Ferguson, viewers learn, is recuperating from back injuries, and he has retired from the police force because of his fear of heights, manifested for the first time during the chase sequence. This second sequence provides other important exposition on the character. He went to law school but has chosen not to practice law. He was engaged to Midge, but she called off the engagement for unstated reasons—she smiles knowingly when he alludes to her breaking it off. Now, he has chosen to quit the police force because of his phobia. The exchanges with Midge also suggest John's limited experience with women and a boyish attitude about them. Midge designs women's lingerie for a living, and when John sees a bra hanging by her drawing board, he asks what it is. Midge's response includes a comment that he is a big boy now and surely knows about such things.

The exposition complete, the film introduces what by conventional definition would be called the main plot of the story. Gavin Elster, an old college acquaintance, enlists Scottie's help in learning what is wrong with Elster's wife, Madeline (Kim Novak). Elster wants his old friend to use his skills as a detective to follow his wife, not because she is having an affair but because her mysterious behavior indicates she is mentally disturbed. Elster wants to know where she goes and what she does, so that he can determine whether hospital care would be appropriate. Scottie is reluctant to take on this sort of work, until he gets a glimpse of Madeline. From that moment on, he is helplessly drawn to her. What viewers might expect of the experienced investigator does not occur; Scottie makes no effort to learn more about Elster, whom he has not seen for years, or the situation that Elster has described. Instead Scottie follows Madeline as she wanders about San Francisco, morbidly, inexplicably drawn to people and places for which she supposedly has no recollection. He quickly becomes entranced by her, and as the events move to a climax, his perspective and his judgment are completely impaired.

It should be said that *Vertigo* is not a realistic film. Unlike *Spellbound*, *Shadow of a Doubt*, and most of Hitchcock's canon, *Vertigo* presents events in a way that defies credibility. The viewer who looks for realism in *Vertigo* is apt to agree with the *New Yorker's* initial review of the movie as "farfetched nonsense" (quoted in *Vertigo* Limited Edition Booklet). *Vertigo* is allegory; it presents characters that transcend the situations of individuals to dramatize states of mind and the human experience and condition. In Jungian terms, John Ferguson is the unrealized self, dissatisfied with himself and unable to act because of his feelings of inadequacy. In Madeline he unconsciously sees a way of completing himself by being united with the feminine ideal. Mysterious and apparently unknowable, Madeline puts Scottie in touch with intuition. Although he struggles to find a rational explanation for her fascination with the past and her strange behavior, he is also helplessly drawn to her. That Gavin Elster is the catalyst for John's search for a whole self is significant. As an old acquaintance, he represents a variation of lost childhood and the self's attempt to regain something lost in childhood, in this case, John's feelings of adequacy (*Man and His Symbols* 170).

Madeline, of course, sharply contrasts with down-to-earth, practical Midge. Midge is simply too real to be desirable to John Ferguson. The film even suggests that Midge represents to the protagonist a negative mother figure. In several instances she refers to herself as "mother." When he is hospitalized in a psychiatric facility after the death of Madeline, Midge tells him not to worry because "mother is here." Jung's anima, however, does not always take positive form. Sometimes it takes the form of a "destructive illusion" (177). This is the role Madeline plays, an unreal image of the ideal that leads Scottie away from reality and to his psychic death. Hitchcock's use of fog filters in the scenes involving Judy/Madeline helps create the effect of a dream, an illusion.

Scottie's vertigo parallels the labyrinth or maze that is often a Jungian symbol of the unconscious and the unrealized self (170). His vertigo is also a metaphor for the skewed point of view that drives his behavior throughout the film. In his debilitated state, overwhelmed by feelings of inadequacy and destruction, he easily becomes a part of the madness within the madness of the film. The fabricated delusions of Madeline, her haunting by the long-dead Carlotta Valdes, are the product of Elster's madness to murder his wife. In Poe fashion the story devolves into a maze in which no point of view is to be trusted, not Scottie's, not Madeline's, not Elster's.

Vertigo uses suspense and mystery to reveal the human quest for wholeness, for a satisfying blend of the real and the ideal. In the film's resolution, which occurs in the mission bell tower where Madeline died earlier, John Ferguson frees himself of her destructive illusion. Distorted by his vertigo, the tower is viewed as a maze or labyrinth. In recognizing Madeline as an illusion, not the ideal, he overcomes his fear of heights and its accompanying vertigo. For the moment he seems to have wrestled down the power of unreason. Whether he triumphs is not certain, however. The final image of the character with arms outstretched, recalling both a crucified Christ and a suicidal Scottie that appears in his dreams, suggests that chaos is still abroad.

Although less discussed than other Hitchcock films, particularly *Vertigo* and *Psycho*, *Marnie* (1964) is an equally fascinating thriller. Nearly twenty years after *Spellbound*, Hitchcock retains his interest in psychoanalysis but reflects the skepticism expressed in the 1960s toward Freud's method. As in *Spellbound*, the mental condition in *Marnie* is integral to both the plot and the theme.

The story takes place in Philadelphia and other locations in the Northeast in 1963. Marnie (Tippi Hedren), a compulsive thief and liar, has been hired by Rutland and Company to work in the payroll department. Unknown to her, Mark Rutland (Sean Connery) suspects that she once worked at Strutt and Company, Rutland's tax consultant, and made off with $10,000 before dyeing her hair, moving to Philadelphia, and applying at the Rutland publishing firm. As he gets to know her better, he falls in love with her. She is fond of him—he has discovered her love of horses and takes her to the racetrack in Atlantic City—but, in addition to being a habitual thief, she has an inexplicable aversion to men. It is her unexpected attraction to him that precipitates a crisis. When she begins to feel trapped by the situation, she robs the safe at Rutland and escapes. Mark tracks her down, and rather than just let her go—if he lets her go, he says, he is criminally and morally responsible—he forces her to marry him, not knowing the full truth of her criminal past and her psychological problems.

The rest of the film is, for viewers as well as Marnie's husband, a discovery of those truths. Hitchcock and screenwriter Jay Presson Allen created in Marnie a character who is believable and consistent. The deeply rooted nature of her illness is dramatically shown in visual and aural details. When she sees the color red—red gladioli in a vase, red ink spilled on her white blouse, or large red dots on a jockey's shirt—Marnie panics and sees red, literally, and the screen, too, is washed in red. Thunder and lightning create a similar response, and she pleads for someone to "stop the colors," although after the storm she has no recollection of seeing colors or being afraid of them. Twice Hitchcock shows her dreaming, and in both instances she hears tapping, as on a door or window, and she speaks and cries out in a child's voice. She has no idea, however, what this recurring dream means. To Forio, her horse, viewers see her extend the only warmth she gives unreservedly to any living creature. All of these details help portray a character who has been deeply traumatized.

In Mark Rutland, the film presents a consistent, but romanticized, figure. He has a detached fascination with animal and human behavior. (The camera has a similar fascination with Rutland, observing him as he nearly obsessively observes Marnie.) When he insists on hiring Marnie—a.k.a. Mary Taylor—his manager questions his action because she lacks references, but Rutland replies that he is just "an interested spectator of the passing parade." The statement is half lie to conceal his purpose, but half truth. His detachment may derive from the fact that his first wife, whom he presumably loved deeply, died very young from a heart condition. In addition, as a trained zoologist, he continues to study animal behavior and to stay current in his field. He has a jaguarundi, Sophie, that he is training, he tells Marnie, to trust him. He has also just written a paper on "arboreal predators of the Brazilian rainforest." After he and Marnie marry and he seeks to understand her, he also studies her behavior, reading books with such titles as *Sexual Aberrations of the Criminal Female*.

Mark's love for Marnie is believable. His desire to protect her, by marrying her and thereby eliminating her need to steal, may seem farfetched, but love has caused people through the ages to do things that others have considered strange. Nor is the character without his own vulnerabilities. After all, when Marnie marries him, she does not tell him that she has robbed not once, but five times over a period of five years amounting to about $150,000. Those facts have not been blocked from her consciousness. Nor does she tell him she is repulsed by men, not until their honeymoon, when she runs screaming from his touch.

The character of Mark Rutland is, nonetheless, romanticized. There is no psychiatrist in this film, and one is not needed, since Marnie's husband seems to possess all the wisdom and knowledge of a trained analyst. One of the most entertaining scenes in the movie occurs one night at Wykwyd, the family estate where the couple lives. Marnie is having her old nightmare; hearing her cries, Mark goes to her room and manages, while she is only half awake, to ask her questions about the dream, which she begins to describe for him. In seconds, however, she is fully awake, and she asks him, caustically, "You Freud? Me Jane?" He does not blink, only smiles and continues to talk calmly about her troubled condition. In a witty exchange sprinkled with psychoanalytic parlance, they argue the merits of her seeing a psychiatrist and reading books on deviant behavior.

Because of Mark's deft handling of the situation, the banter is a tool by which she begins to face her pain. "I don't need to read that muck," she says to him, "to know that women are stupid and feeble, that men are filthy pigs." She tries to stop the conversation, but he continues. Finally, she gives in: "You're really dying to play doctor, aren't you" and "Okay, I'm a big movie fan; I know the games." She suggests they free-associate. He conducts the exercise with emotional detachment and uncanny skill in using words that get a telling response from her. Terrified by the anger and fear the game provokes in her, she admits, for the first time, how desperately she needs and wants help.

The film's dramatic conclusion begins, appropriately in this story about predation, with a hunt. Marnie rides in the hunt being held at Wykwyd and, during a pause, bolts when she spies someone in a vibrant red jacket. She is already under stress because Mark's sister-in-law, suspecting a less-than-savory connection between Marnie and Strutt, has invited Strutt and his wife to the social event, and Strutt has recognized Marnie. Riding wildly away from the scene, jumping fences and hedges, she does not see the stone wall until she is upon it. As Forio jumps, too late, his legs hit the wall, and she is thrown from the horse. He lies helplessly on his side, his belly exposed to the camera. She manages to get a pistol from a neighboring cottage and to shoot the horse in, what viewers soon learn, is a reenactment of a killing she performed when she was only five years old. The death of the horse, the only creature she has loved unquestioningly and, one might argue, a substitute for human relationships, catapults her to the brink of remembering the earlier event. Now in a near trance, she goes to the Rutland safe in an attempt to steal and therefore compensate for her loss. The various elements of her psyche war with one another, however; her hand will not perform what instinct tells it to do. In the final scene, Mark takes her to Baltimore for a confrontation with her mother and a complete revelation of Marnie's past.

Psychologically, the story makes sense. When Marnie recovers her memory, she also castigates herself for her lies and crimes. Mark tells her to have some compassion for herself. "When a child . . . can't get love," he says, "it takes what it can get, any way it can get it." Like a person with a multiple personality, Marnie had created for herself a role that allowed her not only to cope but also to feel some emotional satisfaction.

Both the frequency of mental illness in Hitchcock's films and his serious treatment of it are remarkable. Occasionally he exploits mental illness, as in the stereotypical behavior of the madman seen in *Psycho*, but taken as a whole Hitchcock's films show an overwhelming recognition of and tolerance for the existence of mental illness. It is a part of the greater unpredictability of the world that humans try to control. The chaos that inhabits this world often permeates the psyches of his characters. They, like the world, sometimes go a little "crazy." It can, and does, Hitchcock says, happen to anyone.

CHAPTER FOUR

~

Women Who Can't Forget

In *Sunset Boulevard*, when writer Joe Gillis drives up to Norma Desmond's mansion for the first time, he is reminded of Miss Havisham, Charles Dickens's character in *Great Expectations*. Desmond's mansion, Gillis observes, has been "stricken" with a "creeping paralysis." Dickens's Miss Havisham, a classic portrayal of the scorned woman, lives secluded, shut off from the sunlight in a house long neglected and now surrounded by weeds. Dressed in the bridal gown she wore decades ago when her betrothed jilted her, the gown now tattered and yellowed, she has trapped herself in a past moment and relives that moment night after night and day after day. The parallel with Norma Desmond is apt. For Desmond, as for Miss Havisham, the present does not exist, and only the past is relevant.

Preserving memory of the past is critical to personal development and growth. People learn lessons, reinforce belief in their values, and affirm their relationships with others by remembering and even celebrating their past. Family members pass down stories of grandparents and great-grandparents whose experiences and attitudes form the basis of traditions within the family. People relive their pasts, too, as children grow up to emulate their parents in myriad ways. Whether for good or for ill, human beings remember and even repeat the past. Most people, however, manage a balance between the past and the present, using the past as a kind of rearview mirror that helps give direction, that augments a person's point of view without distracting her from the forward perspective provided by a clear windshield view of the present.

The exact relation of nostalgia—a feeling that the past was better than the present—to mental health is not entirely understood.[7] Certainly, when the balance of past and present perspectives is lost, there is the threat of emotional or mental instability. Sometimes that instability is caused by or exacerbated by other conditions as well, such as depression or even psychosis. In literature and film there are numerous instances of women, in particular, who suffer from this imbalance. Often these characters not only live in the past, so to speak, but also romanticize it. The images and experiences of the past are perceived as the only significant framework for living because they are valued as the only worthwhile or the most worthwhile experiences in the characters' lives. In other instances characters try to deny the past because of the pain of remembering. They succeed only in rewriting it and then living an illusion. Characters who cling to the past as a happier time gain psychological and emotional comfort. First, the past is a known entity, and, when the present or hopes for the future disappoint or defy understanding, fleeing to a memory offers consolation, sedation. Second, as for everyone, memory provides continuity for these characters. Amid what may seem to be the randomness of human experience, however, they become overreliant on the past, looking backward rather than forward. Finally, clinging to the past precludes what should be inevitable: growing up.

Sunset Boulevard, director Billy Wilder's 1950 black-and-white masterpiece, is the first of many notable films that have treated the intertwined topics of women, the past, and mental illness. In *Sunset Boulevard* Norma Desmond (Gloria Swanson) makes the past her only reality. A marvelously successful star of silent movies of the 1920s and 1930s, Desmond, now well into middle age, lives secluded in her Hollywood mansion on Sunset Boulevard, and obsessively preens her image of herself as the great screen idol. Her only companion is Max (Erich von Stroheim), her butler and, as viewers eventually learn, her first husband and the filmmaker who discovered her. With Max's worshipful assistance, the legend is kept alive. He writes fan letters to her, runs her old movies, and constantly reinforces the memories of her former, glorious stardom with the implication that she will be a star again. When Joe Gillis (William Holden), an out-of-work movie writer, wanders onto her rundown property, mistakenly thinking it is deserted, he is both repulsed and intrigued by Desmond. Because he needs the money, he agrees to read and edit a movie script she has been working on for years. He then succumbs to her pressure that he move in, and soon he becomes a part of her make-believe.

Norma has surrounded herself with the things of the past. Her mansion retains its original design and decor, sporting opulent ceilings, floors, and furnishings that were the rage among Hollywood's elite of the 1920s and 1930s. In its size and grandeur, the house dwarfs its living owner while serving as a monument to her past fame. The parlor is strangely populated with dozens of photos, drawings, and paintings of herself during her Hollywood heyday. Her magnificent wardrobe and jewels also date to her past glory days. To Joe Gillis she rails against the current Hollywood, with its sound movies, "idiot" producers, and inferior stars. Viewers get the impression, however, that when she has no audience, she contents herself with simply ignoring the present, wrapping herself in the comfort of memory. Her retreat to the past also suggests the make-believe play of children. In the early sequence when Gillis is led by Max into the mansion, he is mistaken by both the butler and his mistress for an undertaker. The recently departed for whom the undertaker is to deliver a coffin is a chimpanzee, apparently Norma's longtime pet and friend. When Gillis begins to review her script, he remarks on the "childish scrawl" of her handwriting. Later, after Joe has settled in to the household, Norma dresses up and mimes characters from silent movies to entertain him when she thinks he may be getting bored with her.

Norma Desmond's inability to accept her fading fame and the death of the Hollywood she knew is punctuated at times, Max explains, by moments of melancholy and suicide attempts. This inability to accept change extends to an unwillingness to accept anything that shatters her illusion of happiness. On New Year's Eve, Joe rebels against her presumptuousness and the control she has taken of his life. He hints that he has a girlfriend, and then he storms out of the palace. His action, of course, occasions her to slit her wrists. On a very basic level, Norma simply refuses to grow up. By movie's end her psychosis turns homicidal.

Norma Desmond alone has forged her prison. Unlike Miss Havisham's mansion, Desmond's "grim Sunset castle," as Joe calls it, has no bars at the windows and doors. In fact, the doors within the house have no locks, which were removed on the advice of Norma's doctor after one of her suicide attempts. Viewers might be tempted to blame Hollywood for her fate. Paramount Pictures and Cecil B. De Mille, who portrays himself in the film, could be accused of having discarded one of its greatest stars when sound was introduced into the movies in the 1930s. Norma Desmond is a strong woman, however. Still wealthy, she owns property in addition to her home, and she has oil wells in Texas. It is her mental condition, rather than any outside oppressor, that is responsible for her tragedy.

In 1951, a year after *Sunset Boulevard* hit movie theaters, Elia Kazan directed Tennessee Williams's screen adaptation of his play *A Streetcar Named Desire*. Like Wilder's film, *A Streetcar Named Desire* presents a study in black-and-white of a woman whose mental health is tragically entwined with her obsession with the past. Set in New Orleans just after World War II, *Streetcar* follows the deterioration of Blanche Dubois (Vivien Leigh), who has come to stay with her sister and brother-in-law, Stella (Kim Hunter) and Stanley Kowalski (Marlon Brando). The family estate, Belle Rive, in Mississippi has been lost, and, as viewers later learn, Blanche has been fired from her job as a high school English teacher. Both events are part of a downward spiral that takes her, finally, to the Kowalskis' squalid tenement in the French Quarter, ironically named Elysian Fields, the happy, perfect land of Roman mythology.

Drinking much of the time, Blanche weaves back and forth mentally and emotionally between past and present. Time seems to have been suspended for her years ago when her young husband shot himself. Believing that her cruelty and her inability to understand his nervous, sensitive nature led to his suicide, she is tormented by memories of his death and a need to recapture the romance of her Southern girlhood. Words spoken to her sometimes echo in her head; just as often words from the past and the ring of a gunshot echo in her memory. In the urban setting of New Orleans, her chiffon dresses, imitation furs and jewels, and waved hair of an earlier time make her an object of pathos. She shrinks from bright lights, both to conceal her age—as though this were the nineteenth century and a woman in her thirties were doomed to spinsterhood—and to escape reality. "I don't want realism. I want magic," she says to Mitch (Karl Malden), Stanley's friend who has been courting her.

Blanche knows what is happening to her. When she arrives in New Orleans, she tells Stella, "I was on the verge of lunacy." She is lying when she explains to Stella that she was granted a leave of absence from her job and she lies about many facts of her life, but she never lies about the "important things," as viewers come to learn and believe. She says she had to come to New Orleans because "I can't be alone," not only because of the drinking but because of the memories.

The present crashes in on Blanche in the movie's final scenes. Stanley has seen from the start that his sister-in-law's girlish charm and innocence are just a veneer, like the powder she constantly applies to her face to help conceal her age. What she has already confessed to Mitch—that she turned to strangers to take the place of her dead husband, that she even became involved with a boy who was one of her students—Stanley has learned from an acquaintance. His cruelty ends in rape and Blanche's subsequent total break from reality.

At the end of the film, a doctor and a nurse arrive at the Kowalski apartment to take Blanche to a "rest" home. When she realizes that the gentleman is not an old beau, someone she has pretended is going to take her on a cruise, she runs into the backroom, terrified of what her instinct and intuition tell her is to happen. She becomes hysterical and must be restrained by the nurse. When the doctor assists her to her feet and takes her gallantly by the arm, Blanche utters that now famous line, "I have always depended on the kindness of strangers." As she is escorted to the car, her prettiness and coquettish charm are captured one last time in a characterization that became the quintessential image of nineteenth-century Southern beauty and manners faded and corrupted. Vivien Leigh's portrayal of Blanche remains the classic film depiction of the fallen and mentally shattered Southern belle.

Another black-and-white movie shot early in the 1950s is generally underrated, as is Marilyn Monroe's portrayal of its central character. *Don't Bother to Knock* (1952), directed by Roy Baker, is a modest little drama concerned ostensibly with love relationships, but it delivers a portrayal of mental illness equal to the sensitivity and perceptiveness of many other films that show women battling mental afflictions. The movie has two plot lines, both taking place in a single evening in a Chicago hotel. One plot follows Nell Forbes, a mentally disturbed young woman who is baby-sitting the child of a couple attending a conference at the hotel. The other concerns the hotel lounge's singer, Lyn Lesley. Bridging the two stories is the character of Jed, a hotel guest who is also the recently dumped boyfriend of the singer and the man who by the end of the movie helps Nell to begin to deal with the death of her boyfriend. The film occasionally has the flavor of a documentary, evident in a number of other Baker works, as it cuts back and forth between the two stories.

Nell Forbes, played credibly and movingly by Monroe, has been in town only a month, after being hospitalized for three years in an Oregon mental institution. She has come to Chicago to stay with her Uncle Eddie, who operates the elevator at the hotel and has gotten her the baby-sitting job with the belief that she has been "cured." From the start of the film, however, she is troubled and confused. She contradicts herself and lies with great ease, and when she meets Jed (Richard Widmark) she mistakes him for her boyfriend Philip, who, like Jed, was a pilot but who never returned from the war. As she dons the clothes and jewelry of the woman for whom she is working and as she lies to Jed about where she has traveled—Paris—and where she is headed—South America—she shows that she herself wants to be somebody else, to escape reality.

Monroe admirably underplayed the violent element in this character. The movie, too, understates the violence. Nell has attempted suicide, evidenced by one close-up of the scars on her wrists. When Bunny, the little girl she is baby-sitting, hangs out of an open window of their eighth-floor room, Nell rests her hand on the child's back and an ominous expression on Nell's face carries a hint that she is capable of violence. Later, Nell becomes violent: she ties Bunny's hands and feet and gags her so that she cannot cause any more disturbance, and when Eddie visits Nell later in the evening and sees that she is "acting that way again," she knocks him unconscious. Viewers, however, do not see Nell tie up Bunny; that act is revealed later, when the girl is rescued. When Nell hits Eddie, the action is swift; the camera does not linger on the violence. In both instances, Nell is seen not as a person who wants to harm people but as someone desperate to protect her illusion that Jed is Philip and thus to keep him there with her.

Like Nell, Lyn Lesley (Anne Bancroft) is looking for a man who has an "understanding heart." In fact, she broke off her relationship with Jed because he is "glib." In the course of the evening that he spends talking with Nell and getting to know her, he begins to develop sensitivity. At the end of the movie, when the house detective and others have become aware of the situation in Room 809, Nell escapes to the lobby. When the detective spots her and alerts other personnel, he says, "Watch her close. She's a maniac." Hotel guests gather around her and stare. Jed scolds them—this is not a midway, he says—and he talks soothingly and understandingly to Nell, getting her to acknowledge, finally, that he is not Philip.

Norma Desmond, Blanche Dubois, and Nell Forbes all maintain a modicum of order and meaning in their lives by trying to recreate the past. When Norma watches her old movies in a darkened room, she becomes that screen sensation of the 1920s. When Blanche dims the lights and moves flirtatiously about a room, she is in her mind the belle of Belle Rive. When Nell beckons Jed to join her for a drink, she is reunited with her boyfriend. This same pattern is repeated in some later films about women who are experiencing mental illness.

One of the most interesting is *The Rain People* (1969), rightly hailed by Leonard Maltin as a film "whose subject matter was years ahead of its time" (1142). Written and directed by Francis Ford Coppola, *The Rain People* is the story of Natalie Ravenna (Shirley Knight), a young, pregnant Long Islander who gets in her station wagon one morning and runs away from her husband in an effort to find herself. Her trek south and then west is a vague quest for the freedom she knew before marriage. Along the way she picks up a hitchhiker (James Caan), a brain-damaged college football player, who travels with her to the story's conclusion, and she has a brief dalliance with a patrolman (Robert Duvall) who stops her in Nebraska for speeding. Through her experiences with these characters, she learns something of herself.

Natalie seems to suffer from the condition known as borderline personality disorder. Her shaky self-image is underscored by her frequent reference to herself as "she," especially when she refers to herself as a married woman. Her behavior is erratic, marked by mood swings, impulsiveness, and indecisiveness. She wants to return to the past, but unlike the protagonists of *Sunset Boulevard, A Streetcar Named Desire*, and *Don't Bother to Knock*, she lacks a clear sense of self and a satisfying role to recreate. She sees herself as having been independent and free before she married Vinnie, but she was probably never independent and free emotionally. In the film's opening she stops at her parents' home—it is six a.m. and she awakens them—to tell them she is leaving. The implication is that, of course, she would not leave without letting her parents know; the note she has left for her husband is not sufficient notice. They hover protectively over her, but simultaneously they are incredulous that she is having difficulty and handling it in this manner. Once she is on the road, there are frequent calls to Vinnie to let him know where she is and what she is thinking.

During one of these calls Natalie tells her husband that she is two months' pregnant. She says she had to have the telephone between them because she knew the announcement would make him happy. Unsure of herself, as a woman, wife, and soon-to-be mother, she nonetheless feels trapped. This chord is struck from the onset. The morning she decides to leave Long Island, viewers first see her lying alongside Vinnie in bed, his arm draped over her chest. With care and quiet, she slowly extricates herself, barely disturbing the arm that seems to pin her to the bed. Throughout the story she protests the idea of taking responsibility. On the phone with Vinnie, she makes clear that she feels trapped by her role as a housewife. After picking up Jimmy "Killer" Kilgannon and seeing his childlike behavior and helplessness, she repeatedly seeks to rid herself of him, although she fails to do so until the movie's tragic ending.

Natalie mourns her perceived lack of freedom and control of her life. Now that she is married, she tells Vinnie, her day "belongs" to him. She wants to feel she has control, and so she assumes certain socially prescribed roles. The first evening that she gives Killer a lift, she sits in her motel room carefully applying eyeliner and lipstick prior to what is to be a seduction. Not realizing his disability, she invites him in and begins to act out a ritual of games whereby she manipulates and belittles him. She orders him to kneel and pay homage, and in the process she sees the scar on his head and learns of the injuries he received during a big game. She then assumes the role of parent, ordering Killer to go to his room and go to sleep. Natalie assumes the role of seductress again when she meets Gordon, the patrolman. Preparing for a date with him, she sits in her car very deliberately applying makeup as Killer watches. Finishing, she asks, "Does that do it for you?"

While Natalie is on a quest for independence, the film emphasizes her rootlessness. Her destination is California, not for any purpose but because it is the farthest point she can travel west. Her station wagon, that classic conveyance of the American family, is ironically out of place because of the ambivalence she feels about her marriage and her pregnancy. Long shots of her motoring down the open road suggest a comfortable freedom, but her journey is marked by fitful stops and starts either to phone Vinnie or to try to rid herself of her passenger. Her efforts to find a place for Killer result in bizarre, un-pleasant experiences. Instead of self-discovery, the road too often leads to a dead end where she becomes mired in self-doubt and frus-tration. In Nebraska she takes Killer to Alfred's Reptile Ranch, where a job that Killer might be able to handle is available. Alfred's establishment, it turns out, represents the worst of what freedom af-fords—an out-of-the-way place where the owner can freely exploit animals and people, if needed; a place where the rules do not apply; the Wild West. Natalie leaves Killer there but eventually retrieves him.

In the story's dramatic climax, it is Killer who tries to rescue Natalie. She has left him and his bags at the curb for what seems to be the last time, and she goes off on her date. The final scenes show her with Gor-don in his trailer. He wants to have sex with her, but as they become in-timate she senses that he is making love to someone else. She asks him about his wife and learns that she and their son died four years ago in a house fire. As with the development of Natalie's and Killer's characters, Coppola uses flashbacks to show the emotional impact of the event on the character. Although Gordon says the marriage was unhappy, he is desperate, but apparently unable, to forget. When Natalie says she wants to leave, he becomes angry and tries to force her to stay. Killer and Gor-don's young daughter witness the fight through a window, and Killer goes to Natalie's rescue. The story ends with Killer Kilgannon himself being shot and killed. Natalie tries to drag him away as though to get him back to the car, realizing the attachment she has developed for him.

People hope for pleasant weather when they plan a road trip. The morning Natalie leaves Long Island, it is raining, and the dominant early images in the film are images of rain—raindrops on window ledges, puddles on streets, wiper blades moving methodically across windshields. One morning, as she and Killer drive in the rain, he speaks of the rain people that he heard of in a story. They are a lovely couple, she beautiful and he handsome, and they are made of rain. They cry, and when they do, they wash themselves away. By the end of the story, Natalie has learned something about the sad fragility of life, and she has learned something about herself. She has not learned to accept responsibility, however. When she drags Killer's body away from the trailer, she sobs and talks to him, telling him that he can stay with her, that Vinnie will like him and take care of both him and Natalie. Her tears cannot undo the event.

In *Summer Wishes, Winter Dreams* (1973), directed by Gilbert Cates, Rita Walden (Joanne Woodward), too, is a wife and mother. She is a well-off New Yorker and mother of two grown children who nonetheless is on the edge of mental and emotional collapse. She is trying to cope with the recent revelation of her son's homosexuality and his estrangement from his parents. She worries that as a parent she played a causative role in Bobby's chosen lifestyle, and she is dissatisfied with other aspects of her life, including her marriage of twenty-four years to ophthalmologist Dr. Harry Walden (Martin Balsam). Emotionally and sexually repressed, she avoids any physical relationship with Harry. Juxtaposed against this discontent with the present are her nostalgic and melancholic memories of childhood and adolescence, much of which were spent on her grandparents' farm. Frequent use of flashbacks, dreams, and, later, hallucinations highlights this conflict of past and present.

The death of Rita's mother (Sylvia Sidney) early in the film precipitates a crisis. Following the funeral, Rita's daughter, sister, and brother-in-law begin to pressure her to sell the farm, which originally belonged to her grandparents. For Rita such a step would be anathema, not only because she believes the property should go to Bobby but also, and more importantly, because the farm is the repository of sweet memories that she is not ready to relinquish. Flashbacks show her as a child sitting in a gazebo with her grandmother, who reads to her while she eats raspberry jam. On a visit to the farm following her mother's burial, ostensibly to make arrangements with a real estate agent for the sale of the property, Rita climbs to the hayloft and hallucinates, seeing the hired farm hand with whom she fell in love when she was twelve and a half but who died in the South Pacific during World War II. The scene ends explosively when Rita's daughter (Dori Brenner) ascends the hayloft to urge her mother to sell the farm. When Rita refuses, Anna accuses her of hanging on to memories of a past that are both inaccurate and irrelevant.

The story peaks during Harry and Rita's trip to Europe, which Harry gives her as an anniversary gift. The trip causes both characters to confront the past and the role it has played in their lives. As though to signal the thematic significance of the upcoming scenes, a statue of Peter Pan, the boy in James Barrie's play who refuses to grow up and lives in Never-Never Land, makes a second appearance in the movie, in London. Earlier, when Rita and her mother are walking along the streets of New York, Rita sees a photo of the statue in a window, and it reminds her of the time her teacher gave her a copy of the same photo. On the print Miss Tristram had inscribed these words: "Growing up is harder than learning to fly. One requires truth, the other only fairy dust." In London, Rita thinks regretfully, "Oh, Miss Tristram, I turned out so badly, and I don't know what to do."

This story of a woman growing up reaches its climax and begins to move toward a resolution when Harry and Rita visit a battlefield near Bastogne, France, where Harry fought during World War II. Harry, who is wonderfully understanding of the crisis his wife is experiencing, nonetheless feels frustrated and lost in his marriage. The night before their journey to Bastogne, he articulates beautifully his need for continuity and order when he tells Rita why he must go to Bastogne: "I have to stand some place—some place—where I stood before." At Bastogne, in a poignant and nicely understated scene, Harry recounts for his wife how he killed three young German soldiers on the spot where he and Rita now stand. At that moment twenty-eight years ago, he vowed that he would relish every moment of life for the rest of his life, that he would not waste a single minute and would be grateful for every blessing God sent him. Memory of the lives he took that night, however, has always been with him and has had a more traumatic effect on him than he knew.

Harry's confrontation with the past leaves him feeling that "peace has finally been declared." It also awakens Rita to some truths about herself. She tells Harry that she has decided to sell the farm. She is able to see that, as Anna had said earlier, she has been a junkie, getting from the farm a "fix from the past." In the midst of present disappointments, it has provided, through her memory, comfort, continuity, and escape. She also realizes that to continue her life she will need a measure of courage, perhaps equal to Harry's in fighting the war, to face her feelings and express them to those she loves. As Miss Tristram had advised some years earlier, Rita can grow up only by facing the truth, including the disappointing realization that Bobby will remain estranged from them at least for now, and by living fully in the present moment.

Rita begins to conquer her obsession with the past at the end of this very satisfying film. The protagonist of *Plenty* (1985), directed by Fred Schepisi, does not triumph in this screen adaptation of David Hare's play. In the final sequence of *Plenty* the screen fades to white and then to a young woman standing on a hill in the countryside. It is a beautiful, sunlit day, and the woman, British, is talking to an older gentleman, a Frenchman who is working on a piece of farm equipment. World War II has just ended, and she is exuberant with hopefulness. He remarks facetiously that the British hide their feelings, and they agree that that is a stupid thing to do. "But things will quickly change. We've grown up," she says. "We will improve our world." The camera pans the scenery once more and then cuts back to the woman, who says jubilantly, "There will be days and days and days like this." The camera cuts to a long shot as they descend the hill.

The movie chronicles the woman's life in the fifteen years that follow the war, but it is appropriate that the movie end as it began, focusing on her involvement in the war. Susan (Meryl Streep) worked in the underground during the German occupation of France, and the movie opens as she and Resistance fighters wait in the predawn hours for a parachute drop. Sandwiched between the first and final scenes is the character's attempt to recapture the spirit and promise of those days in France. The final sequence of the movie is a bitter and ironic commentary on her obsessive, romantic attachment to those past days.

In the opening there also appears Lazar, code name for another Brit (Sam Neill) who worked in the underground. In the opening scene he is air-dropped into the same field where the Resistance fighters are receiving their supplies. He and Susan spend the next few hours together. They are intimate and share news of home, and then he receives an urgent message over the wireless to move on to Toulouse. He must depart without telling her good-bye, but he leaves her a pair of cuff links given him by the leader of the Resistance organization before the airdrop. Lazar and Susan do not meet again for fifteen years, but in the interim he comes to symbolize for her the ideals of the underground fighters. The tangible emblem of that memory—that nostalgia—is the pair of cuff links that she carries in her handbag.

Plenty is a haunting film that shows in realistic episodes and expert character development the painful progress of a woman's depression. Her life is a series of futile attempts to find satisfaction and happiness. Each effort ends in restlessness and ennui. Shortly after the war, she begins a relationship with Raymond Brock (Charles Dance), a British foreign service worker, and they maintain a relationship for several years, until she decides "it is all a bit easy this way." "Nothing is tested," she says, as relationships and friendships were during the war. "I think of France more than I can tell you. I often think of it, people I met for only an hour or two." She longs for the "great kindnesses" and "bravery" that were evidenced in even the briefest encounters with people. "You could . . . see the very best of them and then move on."

In her work, too, she longs for great acts of freedom and valor. "I want to change everything, and I don't know how," she says. She tries various types of jobs, moving on when each one fails to meet her standards and desires. Educated and brought up among the well-to-do, she is capable, sophisticated, and socially conscious. She is unable, however, to let go of the past and adjust to postwar life.

Throughout her struggles two characters dominate her life: Raymond, whom she eventually marries, and Alice Park (Tracey Ullman), a free-spirited friend. Raymond initially embraces the new world of the late 1940s and the 1950s, as Europe rebuilds and people begin to prosper. With his diplomat's punctilious manner, he speaks for order and the establishment. Alice, on the other hand, epitomizes disorder, freedom from authority. A would-be writer (in great Bohemian fashion), then a teacher of English to foreign students, and finally a self-styled social worker determined to open a home for battered women, Alice follows her passions wherever they take her, even though the road includes a string of broken relationships with married men. While Raymond brings order to Susan's life, Alice serves as her muse, inspiring her to seize the day, not realizing she is encouraging her friend's illusory belief in the past.

Two episodes, in particular, show the influence and conflict of these two forces. The first episode begins in 1952, several years after Susan parts with Raymond. She is working with the Coronation Committee planning the events surrounding Elizabeth II's succession to the throne. Susan has decided that she wants to have a baby, and she chooses Mick (Sting), a merchant she knows only superficially, to be the father. After eighteen months of failing to conceive, she abruptly ends contact with him and rebuffs his attempts to talk to her. One evening when he manages to trap her into conversation, she humiliates him in front of Alice, histrionically lamenting the emotional pain the whole "experiment" has caused her. His frustration and anger erupt into insults as he calls not just her behavior but also Alice's entanglements with married men cruel and dangerous. From a desk drawer Susan withdraws a pistol; earlier, viewers saw her cleaning it during an argument with Raymond. She shoots several times into the wall, and, as is later revealed, she also wounds Mick. The camera cuts to Raymond being called from a meeting to take a phone call. It is Alice, instinctively perhaps, seeking his help in restoring order to Susan's life. The camera cuts again, this time to Raymond making his way through what appears to be a hospital. He enters a room, and the camera moves in for a close-up of Susan as she turns around to face him. It cuts then to a close-up of him and, finally, to images of parachutists descending on a landscape. For the moment Raymond embodies the valor and spirit of those days past. Soon after, she marries him.

In a second episode, Raymond and Susan are living in Jordan several years after she has had another bout with mental illness. While she recuperates, he conducts diplomatic business with the Jordanians. When Alice arrives for a visit, Raymond speaks contentedly of the peace and quiet they have found in Jordan. Slightly embarrassed, he says they have even gotten into playing Scrabble at night. "Susan will never forgive me. Last week I got 'juxtapose' . . . unbelievable—nine letters, including the 'j' and the 'x,' which I'm afraid was on a triple," he smiles.

Tellingly, Alice says that Susan will get her revenge and then, once again his nemesis, Alice questions the way Susan is living—the time she spends resting and the fact that she takes sedatives.

When Susan and Raymond return to London to attend the funeral of Leonard Darwin, Raymond's boss for many years in the diplomatic corps, Susan decides she cannot go back to Jordan. Shortly after, the film reaches its climax, just after Susan has managed to get Raymond fired. When he gets home, she is frenetically stripping wallpaper from the rooms, having decided that the house should be converted into Alice's home for women. Raymond has had enough, though. In pain and anger he confronts her with her refusal to face life and her selfish devotion to the past. The quarrel ends with her running from the room, in the process knocking him unconscious as she slams a door in his face.

The account of her life ends with a scene in a seaside hotel room. There, she and Lazar, who has learned her whereabouts from the BBC, reunite for the first time since the war. The scene parallels the earlier scene, but this time their lovemaking does not affirm their identities and their values or renew hope in the future. She desperately wants it to: "I want to believe in you, so tell me nothing," she says. He suffers the same sense of emptiness, however, that she feels. In his work, in his marriage, and in his lifestyle, he says, he has given in to convention. As she drifts off to sleep, he fingers the cuff links she carries in her purse, and once again he leaves.

Susan's anxiety, sadness, restlessness, feelings of incompleteness and dissatisfaction, and her periodic episodes of losing emotional control are classic symptoms of major depression, as described in the *Diagnostic and Statistical Manual of Mental Disorders* (349–352). Like Norma Desmond, Blanche Dubois, Nell Forbes, Natalie Ravenna, and Rita Walden, she also romanticizes the past to escape her dissatisfaction with the present and to obtain some measure of comfort and sense of continuity in her life. In *Losing Chase* (1996), a beautiful film that premiered on cable television and marked Kevin Bacon's directorial debut, the protagonist, Chase (Helen Mirren), suffers from depression, like some of these other characters. In the opening of the movie, the voice of Chase is heard as the camera focuses on her, seated on the veranda of her family's summer house on Martha's Vineyard. There are, she says, "so many words for a state of mind impossible to describe: clinical depression, nervous break-down, exhaustion, my favorite—collapse." She knows that to her friends on the island "I'd simply lost my mind." There was "a slow, steady decline and, then, bang"; her husband sent her away, and now, after a lengthy hospital stay, she has returned to the island. In the end she tri-umphs; like Rita Walden in *Summer Wishes, Winter Dreams*, she grapples with the past and the unpleasant realities of the present. Perhaps the most significant sign of her improved mental health is her recognition that there will be other storms. That fact is one that Norma Desmond, Blanche Dubois, and Susan cannot confront, and the past destroys them.

These characters all cling to the past rather than accept loss. A number of movies, throughout the decades, have used this theme to depict, not always realistically, the extreme behavior to which a pre-occupation with the past can lead characters. Unlike the nostalgia and depression experienced by some of the characters examined so far, an inability to "let go," especially of love, drives some film women, as seen in Norma Desmond, to obsessive rage and violence. As early as 1947 *Possessed* showcased this fury, making the scorned woman's ob-session the centerpiece of the story. The stereotype has continued to receive treatment in such films as *Play Misty for Me* (1971) and *Fatal Attraction* (1987).

Possessed, while it is representative of the genre known as the woman's film and melodramas of the 1940s, nonetheless offers a realis-tic and sympathetic portrayal of the central character, Louise Howell (Joan Crawford), and her mental illness. Directed by Curtis Bernhardt, the movie begins in medias res, with Louise wandering the streets of Los Angeles, obviously confused and ill. Shortly later, she is being wheeled on a gurney into a hospital's psychiatric ward. She is described by one of the hospital staff as in a "catatonic stupor," and she begins to talk only after she is given medication. From there, the movie is a flashback as she recounts the events leading to the present moment.

The story is this: Louise is a private nurse for the chronically ill and disturbed wife of Dean Graham (Raymond Massey), a wealthy busi-nessman. Unmarried and in her thirties, Louise falls hopelessly in love with David Sutton (Van Heflin), playboy and acquaintance of Gra-ham. Her emotional instability is suggested early. On the one hand, she is coolly competent, even emotionless, as she ministers to the incessantly complaining and suspicious Pauline Graham. Dean Graham tells Louise he admires her "detachment" in caring for her difficult patient. This emotionless affect seems to have dominated her personality before she met Sutton. She tells him that, for the most part, she felt neither happy nor sad and she avoided emotions so as not to get hurt. This cold professionalism and her blank affect contrast markedly, however, with her hysterical reaction and possessive behavior whenever Sutton tries to end their relationship. After several attempts to break it off, he manages to free himself by taking a job for Graham in Canada.

The character of Louise is not drawn or played by Crawford simplistically or one-dimensionally. As the story progresses, she is shown to be both complex and genuinely caring. She eventually marries Dean Graham, after Pauline's suicide, and she becomes a loving mother to his young son, Winn. When Sutton returns and begins an apparently serious relationship with Graham's daughter, Carol, Louise becomes increasingly disturbed. She experiences paranoia and feelings of being persecuted. She hallucinates that in a jealous rage she has tried to shove Carol down a flight of stairs, and she comes to believe that she helped Pauline commit suicide. Her inability to distinguish fact from fiction creates both mental confusion and overwhelming guilt. Her inability to know what is real from what is not real worsens, until she visits, under an assumed name, a doctor to learn what is wrong with her. She is told she suffers from neurasthenia, which she equates with schizophrenia—"insanity," she whispers. Misguided by a sense of shame and a false belief that she cannot be helped medically, she refuses to see a psychiatrist. She becomes more ill, and, when she learns that David and Carol plan to marry, her delusions culminate in her shooting and killing Sutton. As the movie ends, Dean is at her bedside, and the psychiatrist assures him that, although Louise is suffering from psychosis, she can fully recover.

Later box office successes tell similar stories of scorned women who cannot let go of the past. Like Louise Howell, the female protagonists of Clint Eastwood's *Play Misty for Me* and Adrian Lyne's *Fatal Attraction* cannot accept the loss of the men with whom they have been involved. Like Howell, they attribute to these men a deeply felt love and a sense of strong commitment, even though the women have been told there is no possibility of a long-term relationship. In addition, the love these women imagine to exist becomes the one needed thing that fills for them the void of loneliness and emptiness they otherwise experience. Unfortunately, *Play Misty for Me* and *Fatal Attraction*, unlike *Possessed*, are preoccupied with the violence and revenge the characters exact upon their offenders.

Both films depict characters suffering from psychiatric illness. In fact, as Steven E. Hyler points out, both women display behavior and other aspects of borderline personality disorder.[8] In *Play Misty for Me*, Evelyn Draper (Jessica Walter) is a fan of late-night radio disc jockey Dave Garland (Eastwood) who becomes obsessed with him. They spend one night together—"no strings attached," they agree—but she cannot let go. She telephones, shows up unannounced at his place, and in other ways imposes on their acquaintance the language and "strings" of a serious relationship. As he attempts to free himself, she bears down harder, staging a suicide attempt to keep him by her side, stalking him, and, when he has a cabbie drive her away from the restaurant where he is having a business lunch, retaliating by tearing up his house and slashing his maid with a butcher knife. Evelyn's fear of abandonment, her extreme fluctuations of emotion—nice girl eager to please one moment, foul-mouthed tramp moments later when she is crossed—and her uncontrollable anger are graphically portrayed. Her behavior is sensationalized, and viewers are given no chance to sympathize with her. She is presented one-dimensionally as a monster or devil.

Similarly, in *Fatal Attraction*, Alex Forrest (Glenn Close) is depicted as a predator who torments Dan Gallagher (Michael Douglas) and his wife Beth (Anne Archer) and their daughter. Her jealous rage knows no bounds, and the film seems to delight in highlighting the products of her irrational anger—the cuts she inflicts on herself as Beth looks on, the corroded hood of Dan's car after she has poured battery acid on it, a pot of boiling water into which she has placed Dan's daughter's pet rabbit, and her final bloody assault on Beth with a kitchen knife.

Evelyn Draper and Alex Forrest are larger than life. Their menacing behavior is apparently unstoppable, until the final climactic moments when their defeat demands the strength of not one but several characters. By the end of these movies, viewers sigh with relief that Evelyn and Alex have been destroyed. Unlike Louise Howell, they do not gain the viewer's sympathy, and their mental illness evokes no understanding.

The struggle to deal with the past sometimes communicates beyond the character's personal experience, speaking on an epic level about the shared experiences of many. Such is the case in two notable films of recent years: *Sophie's Choice* (1982) and *Beloved* (1998).

Sophie's Choice, written and directed by Alan J. Pakula from the William Styron novel of the same title, deals explicitly with mental illness through the character of Nathan Landau (Kevin Kline), who suffers from paranoid schizophrenia. The movie deals implicitly, too, with mental illness through the character of Sophie Zawistowska (Meryl Streep), who suffers from despair and depression that are directly tied to her inability to confront the past. The story tells of the friendship of Stingo (Peter MacNicol), a twenty-two-year-old Southerner who moves to New York City to write his first novel, with Nathan and Sophie in 1947. Sophie, a Polish war refugee, and Nathan, her Jewish lover, are Stingo's upstairs neighbors in a Brooklyn boardinghouse. The story is immediately concerned with those relationships, but it also tells a tale of the effects of war and racism on human lives and the human spirit.

Sophie frequently speaks of the past. Her childhood could not have been more beautiful, she tells Stingo. Her father, a professor of law and linguistics at the University of Krakow, and her mother, whom Sophie remembers for her lovely piano playing, doted on her. Initially her reminiscences are half-truths, since she cannot bring herself to tell the truth about her father, who was vociferously anti-Semitic and advocated in one of his writings the total extermination of the Jews. By means of three lengthy flashbacks, Sophie's complete story is told. As a young woman she came to hate her father for his anti-Semitism, but she never found the courage to tell him so. Of all her family, however, she alone survived the Nazis. Her father and her husband were, with all other Polish academics, taken away and shot by the Germans. Sophie and her son and daughter were sent to Auschwitz for her minor offense of stealing a ham. She never saw her mother again. At Auschwitz she was made to choose which of her children would be sent to the children's camp and which to the crematorium. Her son was spared, but she never saw him again. After the liberation, while she was in a refugee camp in Switzerland, she attempted suicide rather than live with the choice she had been forced to make.

In remembering and in telling these memories, Sophie does not simply recreate the past. She tries to create a new past. She cannot accept her father for his hatred of the Jews, so she idealizes him to Stingo as "a civilized man in an uncivilized world," "a good man." He used language to foster his hatred, but she fondly describes him as one who taught her the many languages she now speaks. When Stingo learns the truth about her father and asks why she lied to him, she says she lied because she was afraid of being left alone. It is guilt, too, that causes her to deny the reality of the past. She outlived everyone, not only the people she loved but the Jews and all the other prisoners exterminated by the Germans. In addition to survivor's guilt, she feels guilt for her lack of courage, throughout her life, she says. Her sins of cowardice are many: she was afraid to confront her father about his views, she was afraid to help the Resistance when she was asked, and she sees her "choice" at Auschwitz as a failure of courage, referring to it as her "shame."

Yet Sophie cannot let go of the reality of the past, the past she actually lived. She relives her torment and perhaps even relishes her pain and guilt by living the present with Nathan, not only a Jew but a Jew who rescued her, a Polish Catholic, and brought her back to health when she first arrived in America, and a Jew who is obsessed with discovering the full extent of the Nazis' war crimes. Nathan's treatment of her is often extreme and irrational. At times, in a state of euphoria, he worships her as perfection in mind, body, and spirit. Then, seemingly without warning, he mistreats her, verbally and, as his mental condition deteriorates, physically abusing her. Yet, she cannot leave him. At the movie's end, when Nathan descends into a violent rage, Stingo professes his love for Sophie and they take a train to Washington, but she cannot stay with Stingo. She must be with Nathan, she says.

The second and third flashbacks in the movie tell of Sophie's life in Poland during the Nazi occupation. Unlike the first flashback, which recounts Nathan's encounter with her in New York, these two flashbacks use desaturated color. The faded, dull look this technique gives the sequences serves the general purpose of reminding viewers that these are scenes of the past. More specifically, the lack of color helps transport Sophie's story to another plane, showing the larger landscape of the Nazis' crimes. The second flashback begins with an extreme close-up of a portrait of Sophie's father, foreshadowing the destructive impact his anti-Semitism will have on her spirit. The flashback does more, however, than portray one man's effect on a daughter. It shows the effect of Hitler's racism on multitudes of people. Sophie visits the Jewish ghetto after discovering, while typing her father's work, his proposal to exterminate the Jews. Disbelieving, she sees the groups of Polish Jews ostracized and isolated. Later in the sequence, those groups grow in numbers, as she and her children are shown being carried by train with other prisoners to Auschwitz. When, because of her language skills, she is enlisted to work in the office of Commandant Hoess, she must walk past the barracks where scores of naked prisoners are awaiting execution. In the third, wrenching flashback, Sophie must choose which of her children will live, against the backdrop of hundreds of other victims awaiting their fate as they stand on the train platform at Auschwitz. The anguish of her personal tragedy speaks for the tragedies of all those victims.

Perhaps the most intense and disturbing film to treat this theme of women and the inescapable past is *Beloved* (1998), directed by Jonathan Demme from a screenplay based on Toni Morrison's Pulitzer Prize–winning novel. Unlike the other films discussed here, *Beloved* contains an element of the supernatural. It gives the story a brilliantly symbolic and epical dimension that at first challenges viewers' ability to suspend their disbelief.

The story takes place in 1873 on the outskirts of Cincinnati but covers earlier events in Sweet Home, Kentucky, where Sethe (Oprah Winfrey) and her family were slaves. Through flashbacks viewers learn that after getting her children to freedom in Ohio, Sethe herself managed to escape, giving birth to her youngest daughter, Denver, on the Ohio River, the real and symbolic dividing line between bondage and freedom. After only twenty-eight days of freedom, however, her white master came to recapture her and her children. Rather than send her children back to that world, she attempted to kill them. She succeeded in killing the oldest of her baby daughters, Beloved, by slitting her throat. Reviling Sethe as an "animal," the master abandons his mission.

When the film opens, Sethe, her two sons, and Denver, a girl now of eighteen (Kimberly Elise), are living in the home of Baby Suggs, Sethe's mother-in-law, whose freedom had been bought by her son, Halle. The interior of the house glows red at times and is regularly disturbed by a violent spirit that Sethe knows is her infant daughter, Beloved. A friend from Sweet Home, Paul D (Danny Glover), finds his way to the house at 124 Bluestone Road, and after eighteen years renews his friendship with Sethe and then becomes her lover. Somehow he manages to banish the ghost, and for a time the house settles into a degree of normalcy and peace—until the day a mysterious young woman appears in the yard. Propped against a tree and teeming with insects, she seems near death, yet is a robust young woman. It is not long before her identity is clear: she is Beloved, returned from the grave, physically mature but mentally and in her manners still an infant. Denver lovingly cares for her, but it is only Sethe whom Beloved (Thandie Newton) desires. The longer she is present, the more trouble she poses, clinging ever more tightly to Sethe, arousing jealousy in Denver, and eventually seducing Paul D, who leaves because he cannot tell Sethe what has happened.

For Sethe, Beloved is the embodiment of her mother's guilt as well as the only good she can recall from her past. Sethe is haunted by the past: memories of her mother, a slave, being hanged at Sweet Home; memories of herself being demeaned, abused, raped, and beaten by the white men of Sweet Home; memories of her husband's failure to escape with her from Kentucky; memories of being hunted by her master; and memories of the killing of her baby and the consequent revilement by the black community. Although she is haunted by these memories, she also tries to deny them. She never tells Denver, for example, of these horrors. Although she begins to confide in Paul D, Sethe's whole reality once Beloved has driven Paul away becomes the return of her daughter, as though the past had not occurred. Sethe neglects her job and is fired. She spends her savings on festive decorations for the house and sweets for Beloved. As the food and money run out, she becomes ill, more and more disconnected from reality, confused, and delusionary.

It is finally Denver, the timid, lonely, too-little-loved embodiment of a starved present, who begins to break the spell of the baby ghost. With a great deal of courage, she ventures to town, finds work, and enlists the aid of the black women in the community. At the movie's end Beloved has been exorcised and banished, and Paul D has returned to help rescue Sethe. When Sethe mourns that Beloved was her "best thing," Paul

D smiles and says, "You're your best thing." On that promising note, the story suggests that an affirmation of her own strength and integrity will enable Sethe to put the past to rest.

Sethe's madness is not the only madness to occur in *Beloved*. Her husband, Halle, never joined her in Ohio, and for almost twenty years she never knew why. From Paul D she learns that Halle lost his mind at the same time she was being brutalized by the white men of Sweet Home. From the barn loft he witnessed her abuse at the hands of the master's nephews. Pinning her to the ground, they sucked the mother's milk from her breasts. It was the final brutalization that Halle could bear to see.

The supernatural expands the canvas of this story. It is more than a story of one African slave and of one family. The ghost is the manifestation of Sethe's obsession with the past, but it is also a symbol of the complexity of dealing with the past that has faced African Americans. Like Sethe's personal past, the African slave's past in America is unfathomable. Therefore, it must be repressed and suppressed, denied. Yet, it cannot be denied. Beloved's presence is so strong that it obliterates any attention to the present. There is hope for the future in *Beloved* not simply because the black community exorcises Beloved but, more importantly, because the women acknowledge the ghost's existence. The horror of Sethe's murder of her infant, but also the rightness of it, is finally faced.

Memory plays such a vital role in mental health. Remembering the past gives a person direction, strength, and a sense of connectedness to others. The destruction of memory, as in Alzheimer's patients, reduces the ability to function. An obsession with the past precludes a meaningful present and future. In films Hollywood has managed on several occasions to explore, convincingly, the hold the past can have and its relationship to mental illness.

CHAPTER FIVE

~

Divine Madness
Poets, Prophets, and Demons

In various societies and cultures there have been associations between madness and the divine. At various times madness has been linked to possession by supernatural forces, sometimes inspired, sometimes demonic. Even in modern times, amid the advance of science in general and of medical knowledge of mental illness in particular, there occasionally seems to be something inspired, of either a spiritual or a creative nature, about madness. These associations are problematic, however, raising questions about the relationship of mental illness to creativity, mysticism, and even possession. Effective film expressions of divine madness explore the complexities of this relationship or, at the least, acknowledge their existence.

One association often made is that madness and creativity or artistic genius are causally related. Plato believed, for example, that the poet could write best when he was not in his right mind but was, instead, touched by the "madness of the Muses" (Gutin). The association between the two states has prompted study in recent decades of writers, artists, and other creative geniuses and the incidence of mental illness in their lives. Although there are plenty of skeptics who question any relationship between mental illness and creativity, a growing number of psychologists and psychiatrists see a link between the two. Bipolar disease, in particular, has been seen as a condition that encourages artistic creation (Gutin).[9]

In *A Beautiful Mind* (2001), director Ron Howard is concerned, not with issues of causality, but with the seemingly implausible coexistence of serious mental illness and intellectual genius. The by now well-known story of John Nash, a Nobel Prize–winning mathematician, chronicles the progress of both Nash's intellectual and creative talents at Princeton University and his schizophrenia. To communicate the intensity of the schizophrenic experience, Howard depicts the voices John Nash hears as characters in the story. When filmgoers learn that these characters exist only in the mind of John Nash, they begin to realize how difficult it can be for a person suffering from schizophrenia to distinguish what is real from what is not. His total collapse and the subsequent diagnosis of his condition are required for Nash to begin to see the tricks his mind has been playing on him. For the rest of his life he will continue to struggle to resist the voices that call out to him.

The person who has schizophrenia may hear voices but generally does not see people who are not there.[10] Ron Howard might be criticized for taking this liberty with the facts. Enough clues are provided, however, to let viewers know that the characters are imaginary; other students and faculty, for example, never engage in conversation with the characters. More importantly, Howard's technique makes real to viewers a mental condition that is so often mischaracterized as deranged or nonhuman, possibly even violent. Viewers feel connected to and empathize with Nash because of his ability to feel affection for Charles, his imaginary roommate at Princeton, and Charles's niece, Marcee, who calls John Nash "uncle." By making this major symptom of schizophrenia visible, *A Beautiful Mind* does more than most films about this mental condition to humanize it and its sufferers.

Other symptoms of Nash's mental illness are realistically represented, particularly his paranoia and his inability to focus or to discriminate among vast and disparate amounts of data. His whole demeanor, as portrayed by Russell Crowe, indicates a person who, as the story progresses, lives nearly completely in a world of his own imagining and unique ordering. Typical of the misunderstanding and cruelty sometimes shown by the public, when Nash returns to Princeton years after being diagnosed and treated, his awkward manner and gait are mimicked by students.

The depiction of Nash's hospitalization and treatment is problematic, beginning with a sensational scene in which he is confronted at a mathematics conference and wrestled to the ground by a psychiatrist and assistants. Subsequent scenes in the psychiatric hospital of Nash being injected with medication, mutilating his arm as he tries to remove an imaginary code-bearing laser diode, and being administered insulin shock therapy may shock and entertain some viewers, as similar graphic representations of mental treatment have shocked and entertained in earlier movies. On the other hand, the scenes do help viewers understand Nash's refusal to undergo further shock therapy. Like many people afflicted with serious mental illness, Nash also stops taking his medication because of its unpleasant side effects. He believes that he can solve the problem of his mental illness—specifically, the voices—through his own problem-solving skills. Indeed, according to his biographer Sylvia Nasar, John Nash refused to take antipsychotic drugs after his initial treatment (cited in Napoli). The viewer and reader who find John Nash's self-healing unlikely might consider, as one psychiatrist has said, that "every person's mental illness seems to have its own destiny; we [the medical community] can often intervene in it successfully" (Hudgens). Who is to say that a person of superior intelligence cannot will himself to ignore images and voices that his intellect tells him are not real? "Every person is an undiscovered country" (Hudgens).

"That fine madness," a phrase the seventeenth-century writer Michael Drayton used in reference to the poet Christopher Marlowe, of John Nash's mathematical genius is invoked in the title of director Irvin Kershner's *A Fine Madness* (1966), an early cinematic treatment of the topic. In this comic and satiric romp with the Muses, written by Elliott Baker, Samson Shillitoe (Sean Connery) is a struggling poet who has published one volume of poems but whose inspiration is failing him as he attempts to complete what promises to be his magnum opus. He is a misanthrope who must somehow get along in the world in order to make a living, ridiculously as a carpet cleaner. He is a misogynist who does nothing to discourage the advances of women who are drawn to his virile good looks. His arrogant self-absorption is signaled in the opening credits, which scroll over still images of the character's face, pressed in intense poetic thought. His caustic remarks to people he sees as enemies of his poetic endeavors—for example, an ex-wife's lawyer who hounds him for back alimony—are occasionally punctuated by bursts of physical violence. His wife, Rhoda (Joanne Woodward), is needlessly, absurdly, worried that this living ode to Apollo and Narcissus might commit suicide, and she manages to have him placed in the care of a psychiatrist, Dr. Oliver West (Patrick O'Neal), who works with artistic geniuses. Eventually, Samson is admitted to the doctor's mental institute.

The field of psychiatry comes under comic scrutiny and ridicule as Samson battles every effort to treat and cure him. He finally escapes the institute, leaving its staff in turmoil. He manages to pay off his debts, with the financial help of Lydia West (Jean Seberg), the doctor's frustrated wife who has become infatuated with the poet. At movie's end he is still writing and still not conforming. With the new knowledge that Rhoda is pregnant, there is some hope that his angst will be moderated. In Samson Shillitoe, however, madness and creativity will continue to coexist.

Thirty-five years after *A Fine Madness*, Sean Connery again plays a distressed writer in *Finding Forrester* (2001). One-time Pulitzer Prize–winning novelist William Forrester, now seventy, lives as a recluse in the same Bronx apartment where he lived as a young man with his parents and brother. Shortly after the publication to critical acclaim of his first and only novel, his brother died. His brother had survived fighting in World War II, only to be killed when he crashed his car after a night of heavy drinking. Since William had allowed him to get behind the wheel, William felt responsible. With the death shortly after of his parents, he cut himself off from the world. Through the years he has continued to write, but he has submitted nothing for publication. His novel remains immensely popular and is studied in prep school and college classes, but he keeps his whereabouts secret. Finding Forrester has apparently been a preoccupation for at least some of the reading public.

In the story he unwittingly and reluctantly becomes the mentor of a young aspiring writer, a black sixteen-year-old growing up in the Bronx, at times just below Forrester's apartment window and watchful eye, as the boy, Jamal (Rob Brown), and his friends play basketball. By coming to Jamal's aid, Forrester achieves his own redemption. The film recalls Martin Brest's *The Scent of a Woman* (1992), in which another reclusive older man is able to save himself spiritually by befriending a young student, and Gus Van Sant's *Good Will Hunting* (1997), in which a withdrawn psychology professor is able to face his own fears by counseling a troubled young man.

Unlike Samson Shillitoe, William Forrester is not a misanthrope. It is fear, not scorn, that exiles him. As with Samson, however, William's mental disturbance, his depression, coexists with his creativity. Not only is he still able to write, but when forced into human company he is able to nurture another's creativity. William's steady drinking brings the character dangerously close to the stereotype of the alcoholic writer. Although studies suggest a high incidence of alcoholism or problem drinking among artists and writers (Ludwig), their fate is generally less satisfying than William Forrester's. After heroically rescuing Jamal from a charge of plagiarism and expulsion from the elite prep school he is attending on a scholarship, Forrester returns to his homeland, Scotland, and completes a novel before his death from cancer. Ernest Hemingway, American writer and alcoholic, shot and killed himself.

One of the finest movies about mental illness, *Benny & Joon* (1993) captures the poetry sometimes contained in mental illness. Directed by Jeremiah Chechik, the film shows what it is like to suffer from schizophrenia and what it is like to live with a person who has schizophrenia. Besides chronicling the day-to-day frustrations and hazards of this serious disorder, the movie celebrates the creativity and uniqueness of the patient's outlook and behavior. Benjamin Pearl, Benny (Aidan Quinn), has cared for his mentally ill sister, Juniper Pearl, for twelve years, since their parents died. Joon (Mary Stuart Masterson) suffers the classic characteristics of schizophrenia: she hears voices and talks to herself, she has episodic delusions, and she adheres religiously to a routine that makes sense to her and her alone. The impending crisis revolves around the question of whether Benny will at long last follow the advice of Joon's doctor, Dr. Garvey (CCH Pounder), and place his sister in a group home.

Before confronting the crisis, the film revels in the delightful abnormality of Joon's condition. She is intelligent, artistic, and knowledgeable about her illness. When she tries to convince Benny that he is cheating in keeping score at their game of ping-pong, she says, "Don't underestimate the mentally ill. We can count." For Benny, meanwhile, her schizophrenia is simply a part of life. When Sam, a poker-playing friend's offbeat cousin (Johnny Depp), comes to live temporarily with them, Benny explains the situation to him. He tells Sam that Joon's routine is important to her and she hears voices—it "comes with the territory," Benny points out matter-of-factly. In one of the first scenes after Sam has come to live with them, he enters the sunroom where Joon paints and he stares at her. She quips, "Having a Boo Radley moment, are we?"

Joon knows all about the tendency for people not to see the mentally ill as human. Like Scout and Jem in *To Kill a Mockingbird*, people tend to demonize or at least dehumanize people like Boo Radley, who lives in a reality different from that of "normal" people. Joon herself is drawn to different realities, Sam's most notably. A twenty-six year-old who can barely read and write, Sam can nonetheless communicate exquisitely. A master of physical comedy in the tradition of Buster Keaton and Charlie Chaplin, Sam communicates warmth, intelligence, dismay, the whole range of emotions and reactions, through pantomime and sight gags. He mesmerizes Joon, also, with his unconventional and creative approach as their housekeeper, making grilled cheese sandwiches with an iron and ironing board—"Some cultures are defined by their relationship to cheese," Joon says to Benny—and mashing potatoes with a tennis racquet.

There are no simple definitions of normal, this movie seems to say. When Joon first sees Sam, he is sitting in a tree. When she meets him face to face, she says, "You're out of your tree," and he responds, "It's not my tree." Sam has no more control over the way he perceives reality than Joon can control her perceptions. Like the diabetic who takes insulin, they can protect themselves from the danger their uniqueness poses. He does so by taking a job in a video store where he uses his talent to entertain, and she protects herself by taking medications to control those behaviors that can harm her. With these actions Joon and Sam are able to retain the essence of who they are and their creative spirits, their "Poetic Genius," in the poet William Blake's terms ("Marriage" 72). As the story ends, Joon begins to live an independent life in her own apartment, and she and Sam continue their relationship.

In the Australian film *Shine* (1996), directed by Scott Hicks, the protagonist's mental illness is less clearly defined than Joon's schizophrenia. Mental illness, however, is integrally tied to the talents of the character. The movie tells the story of David Helfgott (Geoffrey Rush), an Australian pianist and child protege who battles mental illness and the will of a controlling father (Armin Mueller-Stahl) to achieve musical success and happiness. Even as a boy, when David plays the piano, his performance has an intensity that seems beyond the physical and mental capacity of a child. The piano lurches forward as though leading David, who drags his bench along by his foot and finally stands, literally to keep up with the piano and figuratively to better follow his Muse. As David grows up, his performances, like his commitment to his music, take on the frenzied quality of the prophets described in the Old Testament. Against his father's wishes he studies at London's Royal College of Music on a scholarship and becomes increasingly obsessed with only his music, absent-minded, and unaware of his surroundings. He speaks rapidly and begins to exhibit echolalia; as he repeats words and phrases his father and now his professor have uttered, viewers may be reminded of the prophets speaking in tongues.

The unrelenting tension of the film snaps when David plays Rachmaninoff's Concerto No. 3 in the Royal College finals competition. He plays this very difficult piece brilliantly, but as the music comes to a thundering halt so does David, collapsing onto the piano. What follows is shock treatment and then years of hospitalization in psychiatric facilities. He does not play the piano for all those years, although he never stops fingering imaginary keys and hearing the music in his head. Eventually he is able to free himself of his father's domination, and he returns to music by playing at a restaurant. As an adolescent, David had been befriended by an Australian writer, Katherine Pritchard. She had said that when he played he was able to express the inexpressible, and that it was divine. Years later, when he plays for restaurant goers at Moby's, his performances retain that divine intensity.

Throughout history madness has sometimes also been associated with supernatural forces. In his historical examination of *Madness in Society*, George Rosen notes that by modern standards of mental health, the behavior of the biblical Old Testament prophets would, at the very least, be considered "'borderline psychological states'" (62). Ezekiel, Isaiah, and the other prophets of the Old Testament had visions of the Lord, heard his voice, and transmitted his messages to the Israelites, often in poetic language rich in symbolism and allegory. Like prophets of neighboring peoples, they experienced trances and ecstasies, and spoke in tongues. Often these conditions were induced by music.

In ancient Greece and Rome people believed that madness, whether in creative or religious manifestations, could be caused by divine as well as by natural forces. The ordinary populace regarded mental disturbances as caused by some kind of supernatural intervention. People thought that the mad person was possessed or influenced by a divine power. Even the medical community, which favored physical factors as the source of madness, would rely on a supernatural explanation in cases that defied nature. Plato distinguishes between the two types of madness in the *Phaedrus*, and both Plato and Socrates speak of the benefits of divine madness. Socrates remarks: "'The greatest blessings come by way of madness, indeed of madness that is heaven sent. It was when they were mad that the prophetess at Delphi and the priestess at Dodona achieved so much for which both states and individuals in Greece are thankful: when sane they did little or nothing'" (quoted in Rosen 84).

Even in the late Middle Ages physicians believed that severe mental illness could have either natural or supernatural causes (146). Cases of ecstasy continued to occur and to capture the popular imagination. Christian mystics, such as Francis of Assisi in the early thirteenth century and Theresa of Avila in the sixteenth century, reported seeing visions of God, and some mystics experienced the pains or actual bleeding wounds of Christ's crucifixion, known as stigmata. The behavior of the mystics resembled the trances and ecstasies of the biblical prophets. In modern times, at least one notable psychologist and philosopher refused to discount the mystic state as simple derangement. In *The Varieties of Religious Experience*, William James insists that mystical states exist and their existence "absolutely overthrows the pretension of nonmystical states to be the sole and ultimate dictators of what we may believe" (416). "Rationalistic consciousness, based upon the understanding and the senses alone," he writes, is shown by the mystical state "to be only one kind of consciousness" (412). On the specific matter of mysticism as mental illness, he writes:

To the medical mind these ecstasies signify nothing but suggested and imitated hypnoid states, on an intellectual basis of superstition, and a corporeal one of degeneration and hysteria. Undoubtedly these pathological conditions have existed in many and possibly in all the cases, but that fact tells us nothing about the value for knowledge of the consciousness which they induce. To pass a spiritual judgment upon these states, we must not content ourselves with superficial medical talk, but inquire into their fruits for life. (403)

Ecstasy and hysteria, James says, provide insight about human consciousness. Moreover, whether viewed as being naturally or supernaturally based, madness has been linked to inspiration, with certain positive connotations. It is a notion that even filmmakers have embraced, as seen in such movies as *Agnes of God* and *Equus*.

Agnes of God (1985), directed by Norman Jewison (from the Broadway play by John Pielmeier, who also wrote the screenplay), takes place in contemporary Montreal, Quebec. Young Sister Agnes (Meg Tilly), a novice in a cloistered order of nuns, gives birth; the baby is found strangled in a trash can in her convent cell; and she is charged with manslaughter. Agnes, however, has no memory of the birth or any other events that might shed light on it and her behavior. To complicate matters, she is, according to the Mother Superior of the convent, an innocent; she has lived secluded, first in her mother's home and now the convent, has never been educated, and has a child's point of view and lack of experience with the world.

Agnes shares characteristics of the great mystics. She has visions of the Virgin Mary and of angels, and she is directed by the voice of "the Lady," presumably the Blessed Virgin, who tells her God loves her, Agnes. Like Francis of Assisi and Theresa of Avila, she also experiences profuse bleeding from wounds on the palms of her hands. Twice this phenomenon occurs on screen. For readers who have not viewed the film, these episodes may seem bizarre, unbelievable in twentieth-century North America, but the context of the story and Tilly's portrayal of Agnes make the events believable—nothing less than beatific, as photographed by Sven Nykvist.

Another piece of religious lore is relevant to the story. In both the Eastern and Western churches, St. Agnes is revered as the patron saint of virgins, and she is often portrayed with a lamb, symbol of innocence and sacrifice. According to church history, she lived in the fourth century and was martyred by the Romans when she was only thirteen. According to later legend, a chaste young woman who prays to St. Agnes and performs a prescribed ritual will dream of her future husband on the eve of the saint's feast day, January 21 (Perkins 1173). In the early nineteenth century the British poet John Keats used this lore as the backdrop of a narrative poem, "The Eve of St. Agnes," which evokes both the sensual and the spiritual, blending the conscious with the dream state.

Similarly, *Agnes of God* owes a debt to this legend in its exploration of innocence and experience, madness and sanity. On a night in January, Agnes was directed by her friend, an old nun who lay dying, to go to "Michael," the statue of the archangel Michael that concealed stairs to a passage leading through the convent crypt to the barn. Presumably, on that night in the barn, Agnes's child was conceived, although the identity of the father is never learned.

Into this religious-spiritual-psychological quagmire walks Dr. Martha Livingston (Jane Fonda), the court-appointed psychiatrist who must make a determination as to Agnes's sanity. Dr. Livingston is herself a troubled person. She visits her ailing mother, confined to a nursing home, only to be verbally assaulted with reminders of her shortcomings—a bad marriage, an abortion, and a divorce—and compared unfavorably with her dead sister, who as a nun dedicated her life to God. Like her relationship with her mother, Martha's estrangement from the Catholic Church is unresolved and energizes her investigation of Agnes. Her worldliness is nicely symbolized by her addiction to smoking: on her frequent visits to the convent to talk with Agnes, her chain smoking is a steady reminder of her secular perspective.

Dr. Livingston's study of Agnes—and this unfamiliar terrain of mysticism and religious ecstasy—pits her against the Mother Superior in a battle of ideologies and faiths. The conviction of Mother Miriam Ruth (Anne Bancroft) is that Agnes, like the saints of the past, is "attached to God." Mother Miriam disapproves of psychiatry. Of the investigation of Agnes she warns Dr. Livingston in their first meeting, "I don't want that mind cut open." Mother Miriam's wishes, however, are not pure. She is a woman who has lived in the world; she was married for twenty-plus years and raised two children, although she was a bad wife and mother, she admits in her disarmingly honest fashion. She also smoked two packs of cigarettes a day—unfiltered cigarettes, she tells Dr. Livingston in an amusing display of one-upmanship. Mother Miriam desperately wants to believe in miracles in a world that, she knows firsthand, is devoid of miracles and saints.

In Dr. Livingston's view Agnes is seriously ill. She hallucinates and hears voices, not just of the Lady but of her dead mother, who tells her she is bad, "a mistake." Her spontaneous bleeding Martha sees as the mark of hysteria, and she says it has been described and explained in the psychiatric literature.[11] Martha wins enough trust from Agnes that she is able to learn about Agnes's abusive mother. Through hypnosis the doctor is able also to penetrate the novice's amnesia about her pregnancy and delivery.

In Keats's poem, Madeline and her lover flee the castle, a shadowy world of inexperience and superstition, for the world of experience; they escape "into the storm," the poet writes (1179). In *Agnes of God*, on the other hand, Agnes has fled what she knows of the world and of experience and has taken refuge in the safety of amnesia, of innocence and the dark corridors of the convent.

In "The Eve of St. Agnes," Keats leaves unanswered certain questions: Is the lover real? Is Madeline awake or sleeping? Do the lovers consummate their love? Likewise, Agnes's seduction or rape is left unclear. Dr. Livingston learns when and where it occurred, but Agnes's remembrance of the event, accessed through hypnosis, is both passionate and spiritual. In the dark, shadowy barn she speaks to someone unseen. She asks, "Why me?" Then, lying on the floor of the loft, she sees the doves swooping; she sees "haloes, dividing and dividing," and then "stars falling, falling into the iris of God's eye." The photography of her in the barn, gazing up at the ceiling, the wings of the doves playing in the shadows, recalls Bernini's seventeenth-century sculpture, *The Ecstasy of Saint Theresa*, the angel's arrow poised above Theresa's heart, her face an ecstasy of pain and joy. In the end Agnes lies there speaking of the loveliness, and then, with a sharp shift to the present, we see her hands bleeding. She screams in horror. When Dr. Livingston asks Agnes who did this to her, Agnes responds, "God."

In the end the court finds the young nun not responsible for the murder of the baby, and the judge orders her to be returned to the convent and kept under the supervision of a doctor. The judge has her led from the courtroom when she begins to sing a song that is clearly not religious in content. Perhaps it is a lullaby she heard as a child or the love song of a hired hand, Dr. Livingston speculates. The incident suggests that Agnes's psyche has been shattered, her ecstasy replaced by psychosis. In the final scene of the movie, however, Agnes is shown once again in the bell tower, singing once more of God and love, caressing a dove and then releasing it to the heavens.

Agnes of God leaves unexplained the cause of Agnes's condition. Clearly, her ecstasy is a product, at least in part, of her abuse as a child and recent events, but uncovering those facts through psychiatry does not destroy Agnes's attachment to the divine. In her madness she remains divinely inspired.

While not asking the question explicitly, *Agnes of God* raises a question that is also posed in *Equus*: if madness can create such passion and joy, who is to say that it should be excised? Sidney Lumet's film version of *Equus* (1977), like the play by Peter Shaffer, is disturbing and unrelentingly intense. The story of a stable boy, seventeen-year-old Alan Strang (Peter Firth), who has blinded six horses by gouging a metal hook into their eyes, is difficult to contemplate and at times nearly impossible to watch. What gives the film much of its intensity, however, is the parallel story of the psychiatrist's personal odyssey. Like Dr. Livingston in *Agnes of God*, this doctor is deeply troubled. Unhappy in his marriage and perplexed by the meaning and consequences of his professional work, Dr. Martin Dysart (Richard Burton) experiences his own psychological crisis as he unravels the causes and implications of his patient's unexplainable act of violence.

Dr. Dysart must initially play the part of a detective, questioning and requestioning Alan Strang's parents, employer, and the prosecutor of the case, since the patient himself responds to the psychiatrist by merely singing snips of television commercials, speaking in a peculiarly modern form of tongues. Reluctant to take the case, the doctor has done so primarily because of the urgent pleas of the prosecutor, a friend and colleague. As the doctor's investigation takes him into the psyche of the patient, the journey becomes a personal exploration into his own self.

Raised in a repressive environment, dominated by a mother who is a religious zealot, Alan Strang has divorced himself from reality by constructing a personal religion with *Equus*, Latin for horse, as its god. At once mystic and symbolically sexual, this worship is an outlet for the patient's imagination and passion. Conceived in childhood, this religion/psychosis has become the compulsive center of the boy's life. A stranger even to his parents, Alan Strang can barely read and, viewers are led to believe, has no relationships or even social contacts.

The boy's total, passionate submission to this worship is indeed a madness. The story is told, however, from the point of view of Dr. Dysart, whose life is without passion, personally as well as professionally because he questions the validity of his work as a psychiatrist. He comes to envy Alan for his capacity to give himself entirely to a belief that in one, mystic moment joins the Self with the Other, or the Divine.

Told from this perspective, the story of madness elicits sympathy and empathy from viewers. Since Alan's psychosis is his existence, viewers wonder, with Dr. Dysart, what will become of the boy when he is cured, what will be lost when his sanity is regained. Earlier the psychiatrist, speaking directly to the camera, had described his work with the mentally ill as cutting away "chunks of individuality" for the sake of the god called "Normal." When he finally begins to understand what has led to Alan's violence and helps alleviate the patient's psychic pain, he needs desperately to know what else is excised when the madness has been gouged away. The answer, perhaps, is the passion that has driven the madness.

Equus is as much about the psychiatrist and the state of psychiatry as it is about the patient and the illness. By the 1970s psychiatry had evolved through several stages, from an emphasis on the psychological to concern with social influences and, late in the 1970s, interest in the biological. Likewise, the treatment of mental illness had diversified since the earlier reliance on psychoanalysis. In the 1970s, in addition to the availability of a growing variety of medications, options such as behavior therapy and group therapy became popular and effective. Psychoanalysis with its accompanying emphasis on dream analysis was no longer the only or dominant approach. On a broader level, Dr. Dysart's self-doubts reflect a discipline in flux, a discipline less certain than it had been at times in the past of what constitutes abnormality and how best to help the patient.

In Terry Gilliam's *The Fisher King* (1991), mental illness again is linked to religious inspiration. The movie tells the story of Jack Lucas (Jeff Bridges), a radio disc jockey, a "shock jock" whose casual, cynical arrogance on the air leads a disturbed, lonely listener to go on a shooting rampage at a popular New York City night spot. Three years later, Jack's guilt has driven him into hiding—he works in a video store—paranoia, and heavy drinking. It is Parry (Robin Williams), a delusional street person, who saves him, first physically from a couple of thugs and later spiritually from despair. Ironically, Parry is actually Henry Sagan, formerly a teacher at Hunter College who witnessed the violent death of his wife in the shooting three years earlier. Mentally and emotionally shattered by the tragedy, and clinically traumatized and hospitalized for a while, he has been unable to resume his life and now lives in the basement of the apartment building where he and his wife once lived. For the earlier reality he has constructed a fantasy world of medieval romance in which he plays an honor-bound but often comic and inept knight seeking the holy grail.

Like Sir Thomas Malory's medieval romance, *Le Morte Darthur*, Parry's psychotic adventure weds the power of magic with Christian concepts of redemption and salvation. Voices of "the little people" tell him to seek the grail. The elusive grail is a trophy Parry sees pictured in an architectural magazine that features the Manhattan mansion, a castlelike fortress, of New York millionaire Langdon Carmichael. Parry cannot pursue the grail, however, because the Red Knight, a menacing amalgam of wicked knight and fire-breathing dragon, is always out there. Jack, the little people tell Parry, is "the one," the one who can get the grail. Jack, of course, must first become a believer in magic, and the possibility of redemption.

In Arthurian legend the fisher king figures in the story of Parzival and the quest for the holy grail, the sacred cup supposedly used by Christ at the Last Supper and piously sought by Arthur's knights. The fisher king (in French, *Le Roi Pecheur*, which can be translated as fisher king or sinner king) was Parzival's uncle and the custodian of the holy grail and of the spear that wounded Christ on the cross. Because he has sinned, however, the fisher king has been struck dumb on coming into the presence of the sacred chalice, and from the spear he bears a wound that will not heal. It is Parzival, who has been raised in innocence in the forest (Bulfinch 936), who is able to restore the power of speech to his uncle.[12]

In the movie Parry tells Jack a similar story of the fisher king. As a boy he spent a night alone in the forest to prove his courage so that he could become king, and during the night he had a "sacred vision." Out of the fire there appeared the holy grail, "symbol of God's divine grace," and the boy was told that he was to be the keeper of the grail "so that it may heal the hearts of men." The boy was blinded, however, by other dreams, of power, glory, and beauty; feeling for a moment like a god, rather than a boy, he reached into the fire for the grail. The grail disappeared, and he was left with a wound on his hand. As he grew older, the wound worsened. Eventually life lost its meaning for him. He lost faith in people, and he could not love or feel loved. He began to die. One day a fool wandered into the castle and found the king alone. The simpleminded fool did not see a king, only a man alone and in pain. He asked the king, "What ails you, friend?" and the king replied that he was thirsty. So the fool took a cup from beside the bed, filled it with water, and handed it to the king. As the king drank, he realized his wound had healed. Looking at his hands, he saw that there was the holy grail. In amazement he asked the fool, "How could you find that which my brightest and bravest could not?" The fool replied, "I don't know. I only knew that you were thirsty."

Well into the sixteenth century, when Shakespeare was writing, wandering fools were thought to be not only simpleminded but mad. Thus, it is natural to equate Parry with the fool in his story, who through innocence and kindness is able to make God's grace available to the king. Like the king, Jack must overcome the arrogance that led to his fall and embrace a belief in human kindness and divine intervention. Yet, it is not this simple, for Jack and Parry share the roles of sinner and fool. Like the fisher king, both carry physical wounds from their experiences: Parry has a wound on his forehead that seems to fade but does not disappear until the end of the story, and Jack has wounds on his face and hand from being mugged and later set afire. Like the fisher king, Parry must regain the courage to face life—and his fear of death, embodied in the Red Knight. Like the fool—and like Parry— Jack too is mad. His depression and his paranoia make him almost impossible to understand and love, as seen in his relationship with Anne

(Mercedes Ruehl). In this modern tale of redemption and salvation, then, both the king and the fool are in need of redemption. Moreover, Gilliam's fable says, people must save one another. Whether a fool or a king, whether insane or sane, each individual has a responsibility if the quest is to be completed.

If madness can be divinely inspired, as seen in *Agnes of God*, *Equus*, and *The Fisher King*, it can also be demonic. The ancients thought so. According to 1 Samuel 16:14, "the Spirit of the Lord departed from Saul, and an evil spirit from the Lord tormented him" (quoted in Rosen 24). Rosen explains: "The belief that illness was inflicted by a supernatural power or by an angry deity as a punishment for sin was widespread among the peoples of the ancient world" (28). Hence, the prophet Zechariah prophesies of God punishing those who attack Jerusalem: "On that day, says the Lord, I will strike every horse with panic and its rider with madness" (quoted in Rosen 28). In ancient Greece, too, madness was often defined as possession by an evil spirit or demon, as signified by the Greeks' use of the word *daimonan* (82). The popular notion, through the centuries, of mental illness, lunacy, as tied to the moon derives from the Greeks' belief in possession caused by the lunar deities (82). During the Middle Ages witchcraft was added as a cause of possession by the devil (145). This notion persisted well into the sixteenth and seventeenth centuries, as demonstrated by the many witchcraft trials throughout Europe and America.

This dark side of madness is the stock in trade of the so-called slasher movies and other horror films that portray madness as one-dimensional: violent and satanic. One of its most extreme expressions can be found in *The Exorcist* (1973), William Friedkin's adaptation of William Peter Blatty's novel about devil possession. In a few films, however, the dark side is explored thoughtfully, often as that aspect of mental illness most difficult to comprehend. Most notable among these are *Lilith* and *Sophie's Choice*.

The intriguing *Lilith* (1964), directed by Robert Rossen, who also wrote the screenplay from J. R. Salamanca's novel, explores the relationship of madness both to the inspired and to the demonic. In the story Vincent Bruce (Warren Beatty) is a newly hired occupational therapist-in-training at Poplar Lodge, a private mental hospital for the wealthy. A veteran, home for "a while" now from World War II, Vince has unresolved problems that contribute to his curiosity about and fascination with this hospital in his hometown. He has not recovered from the stigma of his own mother's mental illness and institutionalization, nor has he been able to put the war behind him. Once employed at the hospital, he is easily drawn into the fantasy world of Lilith (Jean Seberg), a beautiful, artistic, and exquisitely manipulative schizophrenic who has been a patient at Poplar Lodge since the age of eighteen.

Kenyon Hopkins's musical score opens to light string music, which evolves into jazz, introducing the tune Lilith plays on her flute and suggesting a Doris Day–Rock Hudson romantic comedy. As the credits begin to roll, watercolor images of butterflies appear. Gradually the bold thick lines of a spider's web are imposed over the images. The images are recalled later, when the hospital's psychiatrist talks to the staff about schizophrenia, pointing out that it has been induced in spiders and other creatures. The webs of such spiders are distinctly asymmetrical, he explains. The playful music juxtaposed against the image of butterflies trapped in webs foreshadows both Lilith and her condition. She is both angel and demon. She first beckons Vincent with her childlike joy and energy, and then she entraps him in her delusions, namely, of herself as a goddess. Like the spider, Lilith weaves, literally; on one occasion Vincent helps disentangle her hair from the loom. Yet, Lilith, too, is ensnared, by her schizophrenia. It creates for her a world of spontaneity and magic, but one that devolves into chaos when limits are placed on it.

So intriguing and groundbreaking about this movie is its suggestion that the chaos is necessary for Vince's growth and creativity. In his passion for Lilith, Vincent begins to address his ambivalence about women. Early in the movie his confusion is summarized in the photograph of his mother that he keeps by his bedside. She had signed it: *For "little" Vincent—Love, Mother.* His confusion is evidenced in his prewar relationship with Laura (Jessica Walter), who has since married Norman (Gene Hackman) because Vincent never made his feelings toward her clear. Later, after he has fallen in love with Lilith, he places her photo next to his mother's. His obsession with Lilith recalls that of James Stewart's character for Madeline in *Vertigo*.

Like the relationship in Hitchcock's film, Vincent's relationship with Lilith soon deteriorates; she engages in trysts with other patients, male and female, and he becomes obsessively jealous. (At one point, when he interrupts one of her rendezvous, she says to him, "I show my love for all of you and you despise me.") Shortly after this episode, he is walking in the rain one night and passes by the home of Laura and Norman. They visit, and later, Laura, alone with Vincent, reveals her unhappiness in her marriage and offers herself to Vincent. He does not respond but leaves. His mental instability is clear in the next scene. At home, he is seen "drowning"—that is, submerging in an aquarium—the doll he has stolen from Lilith's room, the doll he purchased for her at a jousting tournament.

Vincent's love for Lilith, like her love, wants no limits, and the tension created by limits results in chaos. The chaos is first witnessed in Lilith. She extends to everyone her passion or seductiveness, shown in an early scene to be rooted in narcissism when she seems to kiss her own reflection in a pool. At a medieval festival, she flirts with and seductively kisses a young boy. Her behavior recalls the Lilith of Jewish folklore, a demon who threatens newborn children and the first wife of Adam, with whom she breeds demons (Gettings 148). She may also remind viewers of the figure of the lamia, in ancient mythology a monster, part female and part serpent, that preys upon young men (144). In his *Anatomy of Melancholy* of 1621, Robert Burton describes such a creature as consisting of "no substance but mere illusions" (quoted in Abrams, *Major Authors* 1798). Lilith's doctrine of universal love is also illusory. Its magic lasts only as long as no limits are placed on her. When Vincent demands that she love him exclusively, she begins to descend into chaos.

Likewise, Vincent wants no boundaries for the spontaneity that has allowed him to fall in love with Lilith. His love, however, is as illusory as the ideal of beauty and love that she seems to embody. It is noteworthy that they consummate their love after he wins the jousting tournament for her, his lady love, at the festival, a make-believe recreation of medieval chivalry and romance. When he tries to preserve the illusion by jealously keeping Lilith to himself, the tension is too much for him. Together, he and Lilith drive another patient, a young admirer of Lilith's (Peter Fonda), to suicide. Lilith then explodes, destroying her room in a fit of violence, and finally recedes into catatonic silence. In the last, disturbing image of her, she is sprawled on the floor of an isolation cell, staring blankly ahead. In the last images of Vincent, he is first seen walking away from Poplar Lodge. He changes his mind, circles around, stops to face the psychiatrist and the hospital's administrator standing in a doorway, and pleads, "Help me." That is also the final image of the film.

That final close-up of Vincent is not horrific. It is blank. Like Lilith, he has traveled into chaos. He has emerged better off than before he started, for he has experienced spontaneity and passion. He has gone mad, but from the insanity he can begin anew—without the ambivalence and numbness he has felt since the war.

In this film madness is expressed, not medicated or shaped into something that appears to be more acceptable by sane standards. In the very open atmosphere of this resort for the wealthy, there is an honesty among the staff about mental illness and their own connection to it. When Vincent first interviews with Miss Brice (Kim Hunter), he says that he has always been "curious about this place," and when he asks her why she works there, she responds that it is wise for anyone in this field to answer that question thoroughly. A disappointing moment occurs when the staff psychiatrist promotes a myth about mental illness that dates to ancient Greece—it is contagious. The psychiatrist warns Vincent of the danger; throughout the ages, he says, people have become dispossessed by madness when they studied it. Such, he says, is the power of rapture.

At times *Lilith* is disarming because Lilith's schizophrenia gives her power over others, insane and sane alike. Contrary to horror movie depictions of psychotic maniacs in all their violent, demoniac glory, Lilith is physically benign, a delicate work of art like a butterfly. Nonetheless, she cleverly manipulates Vincent by learning his secrets and his vulnerabilities.

That madness can have both an inspired and a demonic aspect is again dramatized in *Sophie's Choice* (1982), directed by Alan J. Pakula, who also wrote the screenplay from William Styron's novel. Set in Brooklyn in 1947, the story concerns Sophie Zawistowska (Meryl Streep), a recent Polish immigrant and a survivor of Auschwitz; her passionate relationship with Nathan Landau (Kevin Kline), a brilliant but disturbed Jew; and their friendship with Stingo (Peter MacNicol), an aspiring Southern writer who also provides narration and commentary on the characters. Sophie and Nathan meet when she collapses in the public library, deathly ill of scurvy, anemia, and other maladies caused by her wretched existence before arriving in New York. A chemist, Nathan tells Sophie, he nurses her back to health. Their friendship with Stingo begins when he moves into Yetta Zimmerman's boardinghouse, where they share rooms.

Sophie calls Nathan's finding her "a miracle." Indeed, he seems to have been touched by the divine. Stingo is impressed by the breadth and depth of Nathan's reading and knowledge, and he brings a poetic magic to Sophie's life. Time spent with Nathan is unpredictable and unconventional. On Sundays he and Sophie dress up in period costumes, to avoid looking like everyone else, he says; and a day the three of them spend at Coney Island is pure, childlike joy and pleasure. The grandeur of the character and his inspiration is captured in a scene in which the trio celebrates Stingo's talent. Nathan has confiscated and read the manuscript of a novel Stingo is writing. Nathan has directed Sophie to take Stingo to a movie while Nathan reads the manuscript. When Sophie and Stingo return, Nathan leads them on a march to the Brooklyn Bridge, where he pulls champagne and glasses from a satchel, climbs a lamp pole on the bridge, salutes the great American writers who stood on that bridge—Walt Whitman, Thomas Wolfe, Hart Crane—and welcomes Stingo "into that pantheon of the gods," toasting him as America's newest voice. It is little wonder, Stingo tells viewers, that he was hopelessly infatuated with this person of such "generous mind," such "a life-enlarging mentor," someone so "utterly, fatally glamorous."

Even as Stingo speaks, however, the camera moves up and away from the characters. They are dwarfed by the Brooklyn Bridge and the city, and the epic quality that Nathan tries to give life is shown to be delusive. Just as he can be brilliant, at times he seems to be possessed by a demon. When this dark spirit overcomes him, he becomes irrationally jealous of attention Sophie shows anyone else, and he is condescending, insulting, and ugly not only to her but to Stingo. This side of Nathan is the first aspect of the character that the film presents. Stingo has just moved in, and he hears the loud quarreling of the lovers. On the stairway Nathan snarls a long litany of foul-mouthed insults first at Sophie, then at Stingo, and leaves the building. Hours later, when he returns and reconciles with Sophie, he says, "Don't you see . . . we are dying." The truth of his words is verified at story's end. Nathan and Sophie try to deny reality by creating a world of make-believe. They call Yetta Zimmerman's boarding house the "Pink Palace" because inside and out it is coated with pink paint, gallons and gallons of it that Yetta's late husband got at a good price from navy surplus. Here in this gingerbread house, the lovers dress up and pretend to be other people, and, most importantly, keep their secrets from each other. Stingo learns Nathan's secret from Nathan's brother, that Nathan suffers from paranoid schizophrenia. Eventually Stingo learns Sophie's secret, too, the secret that underlies the terrible guilt she feels as a survivor of the Nazis. When reality crashes in on Nathan and Sophie, they deny it by committing suicide.

Associations of mental illness with inspiration, creativity, even the supernatural, will probably continue. In *Cross Creek* (1983), directed by Martin Ritt and based on the memoirs of Marjorie Kinnan Rawlings, American writer and author of *The Yearling*, the central character (Mary Steenburgen) has bought, sight unseen, an orange grove in the Florida backwoods. A divorce in process and nothing but a ramshackle cottage and untended grove to her name, she is determined to live on her own as a writer. Cross Creek is harsh swamp country, inhospitable to people and defiant of social conventions. In meeting her for the first time, Norton Baskin (Peter Coyote) says, "You've got to be a little crazy to live out at the Creek." Indeed, her outlook is out of tune with the urban society in which she has been raised. Like the poets and prophets before her, she experiences reality differently and, in turn, she brings a different perspective to conventional reality.

CHAPTER SIX

~

War

A Battle for the Mind and Spirit

The British poet Wilfred Owen fought and died in World War I, and wrote of the horrors of war. In one poem he warns against spreading the "old Lie": "Dulce et decorum est / Pro patria mori" (1846), or "It is sweet and honorable to die for one's country," words originally penned by the ancient Roman poet Horace, who, ironically, wrote during the great Augustan age of peace. To counteract the lie, Owen creates images of young soldiers aging prematurely from starvation and fatigue and dying horrendous deaths from poison gas and gunfire. Other writers have described the realities of war, perhaps most notably Erich Maria Remarque in his novel *All Quiet on the Western Front*. In the movies likewise, there have been efforts to depict war realistically. Among those realities are the various relationships between war and madness or, at the least, the effects of war on mental health.

William Wyler's *The Best Years of Our Lives* (1946) is one of the best early movies about war and remains a classic about the effects of combat on the mind and spirit. Adapted by Robert Sherwood from a novel by MacKinlay Kantor, the film tells the story of three servicemen returning from World War II and trying to readjust to civilian life in their hometown of Boone City. Sergeant Al Stephenson (Fredric March) feels restless, out of touch with his family, and discontented with the prospect of resuming his job at the local bank. His frustration grows when he becomes head of the loan department and must battle the bank's president and officers to win loans for deserving but penniless veterans. Captain Fred Derry (Dana Andrews), decorated for valor, has high hopes of improving his station in civilian life, but he is soon disillusioned by his inability to land a decent-paying job and his loveless marriage. In addition, he is troubled by flashbacks and nightmares of his war experiences as an air bomber. Homer Parrish (Harold Russell), a young sailor who has lost both his hands, struggles emotionally with his disability. All three characters experience emotional difficulty, but it is Derry who is debilitated by a mental condition, what today would likely be called posttraumatic stress disorder, as described in the *Diagnostic and Statistical Manual of Mental Disorders* (463–464).

Derry's condition is portrayed without melodrama. The night of their return to Boone City, Al and Fred get drunk hopping from one bar to another, and Fred ends up sleeping in the Stephensons' apartment. In the middle of the night, the Stephensons' grown daughter, Peggy (Teresa Wright), is awakened by the tormented sounds of Fred's dreaming. Later in the film, as he sits in the nose of a bomber that is headed for the scrap heap, he has a flashback to his days as a bomber. In neither scene is the past depicted on the screen. Its horror is evoked effectively, however, in Derry's face and eyes.

The reaction of Fred's wife, Marie, to his nightmares makes her a plausible foil to Peggy, and it contrasts opposing views of mental illness. Peggy, who has worked for the past two years at a local hospital, is compassionate and competent in her response. Her concern is clear but understated. Marie (Virginia Mayo), on the other hand, seems to lack any awareness of his condition or sympathy toward his pain. Her response to warrior experience is materialistic, shallow. She is quite simply embarrassed by and ashamed of his inability to readjust. This outright acknowledgment of the stigma so often attached to mental illness makes *The Best Years of Our Lives* truly remarkable for its time.

Parrish finds peace and hope through the unrelenting devotion of the girl next door, Stephenson by acting as a momentary hurdle to his daughter's infatuation with Fred Derry, whose alienation from all and everything is the readjustment blues in march time. Derry seeks the milk of human kindness, at least for recuperation. Each character finds balance by interacting, but their suffering continues, like many veterans' mental illnesses. A captain, a sergeant, and a lowly swabie all have their pains fuzzed by the double focus of civilian and military experience.

The effects of war on mental health and the stigma of mental illness are treated more extensively in *The Caine Mutiny* (1954), directed by Edward Dmytryk. Another World War II classic, *The Caine Mutiny* was adapted by Stanley Roberts from Herman Wouk's Pulitzer Prize novel about a fictitious naval mutiny set in 1944 Pearl Harbor. Captain Queeg (Humphrey Bogart) has seen considerable combat before being assigned to the command of the USS *Caine*, a destroyer/mine sweeper. It does not take long for his executive officer, Lieutenant Steve Maryk (Van Johnson), and other crew members to notice his nervous, erratic behavior. In the movie's powerful climax, Queeg panics during a savage typhoon and is unable to function. Maryk takes over the command and is able to save the ship. Queeg subsequently has Maryk court-martialed, and the rest of the movie focuses on the trial.

Queeg's behavior on the *Caine* unquestionably reflects his disturbed, unstable state of mind. His rigid thinking, dramatic mood swings, and paranoia cause him to alienate his crew and to lower its morale, and they impair his professional judgment. In one seriocomic episode he has the men search in the middle of the night for a quart of strawberries he is convinced has been stolen. In a mock heroic scene, the naval leader illogically substitutes sand for strawberries in a vainglorious attempt to convince his followers that his mastery of mathematics, physics, and warfare strategies is the culmination of experience and thought. He suffers from chronic headaches, and as he becomes increasingly nervous and obsessive he more frequently extracts a set of steel balls from his pocket, and rolls and fingers them in his hand.

Considerable discussion occurs onboard the *Caine* as to whether Queeg is a man simply fatigued by war, a coward or an incompetent, or someone who is indeed mentally sick. These discussions foreshadow the courtroom debate that occurs during the trial. The position of the military brass is denial. The navy psychiatrist engages in semantic puzzles, acknowledging that Queeg exhibits a "paranoid personality" but rejecting the idea that the commander is mentally ill. The implication is that mental illness is incompatible with military command: if Captain Queeg were mentally ill, he would not be a navy commander. Maryk's defense attorney, Barney Greenwald (Jose Ferrer), however, is able to break Captain Queeg down during testimony, and Queeg demonstrates in the courtroom some of the symptoms his crew witnessed aboard ship. In the end, Maryk is found innocent of mutiny, but some question remains as to whether Queeg is ill or whether his crew failed him by not giving him the emotional support he needed. Not co-incidentally, the movie is dedicated to the U.S. Navy.

This conflict between the military code and mental health awareness occurs again in the World War II comedy-drama *Captain Newman, M.D.* (1963), directed by David Miller and based on a novel by Leo Rosten. The year is 1944, and psychiatrist Captain Josiah Newman (Gregory Peck) is commander of the neuropsychiatric unit of a stateside army hospital, battling shortages in supplies and staff, bureaucracy, and ignorance about mental illness. The conflict is introduced early. There has been an "alarming increase in neuropsychiatric cases." Early in the war, Newman explains, soldiers suffering acute anxiety and other symptoms were not considered sick. "No mollycoddling" was tolerated in the air corps, and the men were quickly sent back to duty. "Now they're streaming back," he says. He is given six weeks to return them to duty, discharge them, or have them transferred to a permanent hospital. If he delays, "all hell breaks loose." Evidence of the army's lack of patience with these cases occurs when the base commander storms into the office of Newman's commanding officer, ranting that Ward 7 has the "lowest return to duty rate in the entire area command." Later, the base commander makes clear that he regards the patients of Ward 7 not as casualties but as cowards.

A variety of patients populates Ward 7. Several of them manifest the hysteria associated with shell shock, but the audience is drawn into the plight of three patients in particular. In these cases the story is concerned not only with the mental illness of the servicemen but also with the circumstances that helped create it. Colonel Norville Bliss (Eddie Albert), "one of the most brilliant tacticians fighting the air war in the Pacific," has been admitted by Newman, amid the base commander's protests, for observation because of disruptive, obsessive behavior he recently displayed at the officers' club. The condition of Colonel Bliss worsens: he becomes violent and then dissociates into two personalities, in blissful denial of his most recent war experience. He is unable to deal with the guilt he feels for having ordered his men into a battle that took all their lives. Corporal Jim Tompkins (Bobby Darin), who has been decorated for more than thirty bombing missions, drinks excessively and suffers from insomnia and stomach pains. Like Colonel Bliss, Jim Tompkins is struggling with his feelings of guilt. He feels responsible for the death of a buddy he was unable to save when their plane was hit and then crashed and exploded. Captain Paul Winston (Robert Duvall), who was missing in action for thirteen months in France, is nearly catatonic, noncommunicative and motionless. He hid in a cellar during those thirteen months, and as Newman learns, Winston regards himself as a coward and cannot face that reality.

The suffering of Colonel Bliss, Corporal Tompkins, and Captain Winston poignantly refutes the base commander's contention that the men of Ward 7 are not ill. Their conditions are believable, and their stories are moving. Decades after its production, *Captain Newman, M.D.* can still foster awareness of mental illness.

Like *The Best Years of Our Lives*, *The Man in the Gray Flannel Suit* (1956), directed by Nunnally Johnson and scripted by Johnson from a novel by Sloan Wilson, depicts a World War II veteran's difficult readjustment to civilian life. In an engaging subplot, the story also focuses on the public's lack of awareness of mental illness in general, thus reflecting the birth of the community mental health movement in the United States in the 1950s. In 1955 Tom Rath (Gregory Peck) gets a $10,000-a-year public relations job at United Broadcasting Corporation (UBC) on Madison Avenue. In his gray flannel suit, Rath is dressed for the part—of the bright, young family man seeking the American dream of money and success. As the title suggests, the movie primarily concerns the pursuit of this dream. The obstacles are the character's disillusionment with what the dream represents and his failure to put his war experiences of ten years earlier behind him.

Tom and wife Betsy (Jennifer Jones) have three children, a modest home in Connecticut, and a tenuous happiness. She wants them to get ahead, but he is intent just on making ends meet. It is her discontent with their situation that motivates him to take the job at UBC. She complains that "ever since the war," theirs has not been a happy house. She believes that the war is not over for him and that he has changed: he seems far away sometimes, and he has lost the drive and courage he had before he fought in the war. Tom professes to be happy, but memories of the war dog him. Staring at the back of a stranger's neck as he rides the train into the city prompts a flashback to a German soldier's fur collar. On a winter's night in France, Captain Rath killed the soldier to get his coat. Another memory is from fighting in the Pacific, where his unit was sent after Europe. In heavy fighting he is launching grenades, and one of them hits and kills his best friend. Unable to accept what has happened, he carries the body from one medic to another until, finally, a soldier understands the situation and agrees to get help for the wounded friend. The lengthiest flashbacks are to the affair he had during the few months he was stationed in Rome before leaving for the Pacific.

The despair of the war, the conviction that he would not survive, led him into the affair even though he was already married to Betsy. That despair continues to drain him of passion and energy. Like a Hemingway hero, he goes through the motions of living, but war and death have eroded his spirit. His past collides with the present when he learns that he has a son in Italy and he must make several decisions, including whether to tell his wife.

Tom's internal struggle is echoed in his new job at UBC. In tandem with the crisis playing out in his personal life is the challenge he faces at work. As a special assistant to UBC's head, Ralph Hopkins (Fredric March), Tom is helping to launch a national campaign to improve mental health. The program is a personal project of Ralph's, a way for an extremely wealthy and influential man to do "tremendous good." He calls it a "holy cause" and speaks quite informatively of the scope of the problem of mental illness in America. More hospital beds are occupied by the mentally ill, he tells Tom, than by patients of several major physical diseases combined.

How to approach the medical community with this campaign is the challenge. The senior PR executives are stereotypical yes-men, telling Hopkins what they think he wants to hear. Tom must choose between defending the approach he believes will work and going along with what Hopkins and the others have outlined. He must choose between being honest and being slick, between possibly losing his job and achieving success on Madison Avenue. Many of the choices he made during the war were for his physical survival; this time the choice is more complicated—it is for his spirit.

Mental health was a timely issue in 1956, when community-based clinics were first being discussed. In fact, one of Tom Rath's suggestions is that Hopkins's program include such clinics as well as preventive measures. But mental health is more than mere scenery or a prop in this movie. As Tom resolves the conflicts in his personal and professional lives, he takes actions that help insure his own mental and emotional health. Unlike Hemingway's postwar protagonists, this hero wins the battle for his soul.

The emotional and mental complexities veterans face in returning to civilian life are dramatized in a number of movies of the 1970s, 1980s, and 1990s. In *Coming Home* (1978), directed by Hal Ashby, and *Born on the Fourth of July* (1989), directed by Oliver Stone, Vietnam veterans (played by Jon Voight and Tom Cruise, respectively) also deal with the catastrophic physical injuries they incurred in combat. In *Coming Home*, a marine officer (Bruce Dern) survives war only to commit suicide when he returns home. The emotional turmoil these veterans face in reassimilating into American society is compounded by their own ambivalence about the war as well as by the hostility they encounter from Americans. In both Ashby's and Stone's movies, the protagonists work through their anger, resentment, and depression to become opponents of the war.

The true story of Marine Sergeant Ron Kovic as told in *Born on the Fourth of July* is particularly effective in showing the ironies of war. America of the 1950s and early 1960s shaped the attitudes and values of young men who felt duty-bound, like Kovic, to go to Vietnam for their country. The frustration and pain Kovic experiences in returning to a divided nation are captured poignantly in images that trace the changing definitions of patriotism in those years. The opening images of Kovic as a boy playing war with his friends, followed by scenes from a July 4, 1956, parade in his hometown of Massapequa, Long Island, emphasize the glamour and heroism evinced by the marching veterans of World War II, so recently returned as victors from a glorious struggle. Years later, when Kovic himself has returned from war, paralyzed and confined to a wheelchair, he rides in a convertible in Massapequa's Fourth of July parade, but this time he is the one who, like those World War II veterans in 1956, winces at the sounds of the fireworks. As he looks into the crowd of spectators, he sees not a uniform sea of shining patriots but blank stares and, worse, the angry faces of protesters yelling obscenities at him.

Chattahoochee (1990), directed by Mick Jackson, presents in its opening scenes one of the most compelling portrayals of a veteran unable to adjust to civilian life. Three years after fighting in Korea, decorated veteran Emmet Foley (Gary Oldman) suffers a complete mental breakdown, largely as a result of postcombat stress. The film opens with black-and-white footage, a caption that reads "Korea, 1952, 38th Parallel," and the hymn "Jesus Loves Me" playing softly in the background. A close-up of the Oldman character firing his rifle is accompanied by voice-over narration. The character says that coming back a "certified hero" raises people's expectations, "makes 'em think you're a big guy." The camera cuts to 1955, and the film turns to color. From billboard images, the camera makes its way to the interior of a house in a small-town Florida neighborhood. Close-ups of wall hangings parade leisurely before viewers: a needlework display stating "Blessed are the meek," a photograph of Foley in military uniform standing beside a jeep, and framed medals. Finally, the camera turns to Foley and in the next few moments records his frenzied breakdown as he loads a handgun, runs outside shooting at streetlights, parked cars, and other inanimate objects, and yells for someone to call the police. He runs several times between the interior of the house and the yard, perspiring profusely, gulping down glasses of water, muttering that he's "gotta provide for 'em." Once the police arrive and it becomes clear to Foley that they are not going to shoot him, he turns the gun on himself.

Emmet Foley's plan was to be killed by the police so that his wife would receive insurance money. His failed plan is fraught with irony. He survives his suicide attempt and is sent to the Chattahoochee State Mental Hospital, where he will have to fight perhaps harder than ever in his life to survive. Chattahoochee is a filthy, bug-infested warehouse for the mentally ill, indigents, and inmates transferred from the state's overcrowded prisons. Unfortunately, when the movie's setting shifts to Chattahoochee, unity of action and of theme is lost. The movie's focus turns from Emmet's troubled mental state to the deplorable conditions of life at Chattahoochee. The psychological and emotional struggle of Emmet Foley, Korean War veteran, is subordinated to the story of hospital/prison reform.

Perhaps no topic raises questions about the nature and causes of madness as powerfully as war does, and anyone who thinks mental illness has nothing to do with the average person need only view some of the war films made since the 1970s. Repeatedly these films show a wide-ranging variety of characters breaking, to a variety of degrees, under the stress of combat and militarism. "We all go a little mad sometimes," Norman Bates says in *Psycho*. Even the lowliest infantryman can be motivated to discard the rules of war and turn randomly violent, as in *Saving Private Ryan* (1998). In Steven Spielberg's story of World War II during the D-day invasion of 1944, several of the men under the command of Captain John Miller (Tom Hanks) must be held back from killing a German soldier they have captured. In *Platoon* (1986), Oliver Stone's classic Vietnam War film, the protagonist, Chris Taylor (Charlie Sheen), toys with the impulse toward random violence when he torments a Vietnamese villager, and later he succumbs to the impulse when he shoots a member of his own platoon, Sergeant Barnes (Tom Berenger), who has been an antagonist throughout the story. Ironically, Barnes had come to personify violence. In the name of winning the war and motivated by blind hatred of the enemy, Barnes justified shooting, point-blank, a village woman who would not give him the information he wanted. Later, he murdered the sergeant (Sergeant Elias, played by Willem Dafoe) who served as his foil and who had vowed to have charges brought against him.

Other characters dissociate from the reality of combat and become incapable of functioning as soldiers. In *The Thin Red Line* (1998), Terrence Malick's masterful film about the invasion of Guadalcanal during World War II, Sergeant McCron (John Savage) becomes lost in a philosophical miasma following the deaths of all twelve men in his squad. Confused and spent, he sinks to the ground and studies his dog tags, as though to learn or to confirm his identity. Enraged, he pulls handfuls of dirt and grass from the hillside where men are being slaughtered by Japanese gunfire, and he cries that this, the dirt and the grass, is all they are fighting for. He denounces the insanity of the battle, and others in the platoon take his rifle from him. Later, he is heard and seen calling out to no one in particular, perhaps God, asking who decides who will die. Helplessly he asks, Why not me?

The most dramatic and disturbing portrayals of dissociation are still to be found in *The Deer Hunter* (1978), directed by Michael Cimino, and *Full Metal Jacket* (1987), directed by Stanley Kubrick. Both films are artistic depictions of Vietnam War situations. Cimino's film tells the story of three friends, steelworkers in Clairton, Pennsylvania, tracing their lives from the days immediately preceding their induction into the U.S. Army, through combat and imprisonment in Vietnam, to the days following their military service. The protagonist, Michael (Robert De Niro), survives the war, changed but mentally and physically whole. Steven (John Savage) survives but loses both legs. Nick (Christopher Walken), however, does not survive. He is a casualty not of physical injuries incurred during combat but of severe mental illness.

Before his war experience, Nick is shown to be a person who enjoys living in the moment. He is spontaneous, not afraid of his feelings, and not ashamed of showing compassion; but he avoids conflict, serving at times as a peacemaker among the larger group of friends. Unlike his buddy Michael, he enjoys deer hunting not for the hunt but for the trees and the mountains. He also appreciates the element of chance in life. He enjoys betting on little everyday gambles: whether Michael can get the car around a transport truck in barely passable space or whether a particular team will win the game being televised in a friend's bar. Nick is not especially articulate nor does he, like Michael, plan his actions. He simply lives.

Nick's experience in a North Vietnamese prison camp forever robs him of his sense of reality. All three of them—Michael, Nick, and Steven—have been captured and are being held in a cell where they stand in waist-high river water. Above them, the North Vietnamese force prisoners, both U.S. and South Vietnamese soldiers, into a relentless, barbarous game of Russian roulette. A gun is loaded with one bullet and then passed back and forth between two prisoners. As first one prisoner and then the other aims the gun at his temple, bystanders bet on when the bullet will reach the firing chamber. Prisoners who refuse to play are thrown into "the pit," a completely submerged, rat-infested cage allowing only enough space at the surface for the men to breathe. Michael devises a plan whereby he convinces the captors to increase the number of bullets in the gun, and then to allow him and Nick to play each other. Michael's plan is to turn the gun on their captors and to make their escape. He is successful, but only after he and Nick play a grueling, a maddening, game of chance. Both escape the bullets, but Nick becomes hysterical. Once out of the prison, they come close to being rescued by a U.S. Army helicopter, but only Nick is pulled to safety. Mike and Steven cling desperately to the helicopter, but when Steven can no longer hold on, Mike also releases his hold. Nick's confusion and despair deepen as he sees them falling into the river.

Nick is next seen in a Saigon army hospital. Visibly traumatized, he looks at the photograph of his girlfriend he carries in his wallet and then gazes at another patient, whose arms are bandaged, bloodied stumps. When a military doctor interviews Nick, he tries to answer the questions, but, fighting back tears, he is virtually mute. Nonetheless, the doctor releases him. ("We're gonna have to get him out of here," the doctor tells a nurse.) Nick wanders the streets of Saigon aimlessly, once mistaking someone for Michael. Soon he is drawn by sights of bodies being dumped in an alley and by sounds of guns being fired to the same game of chance he had witnessed as a prisoner. The game is being played in a backroom, but the scene is in most ways a mirror image of the earlier scene. Two players sit across from each other at a table while gamblers crowd around. Nick angrily grabs the gun, and first fires it at one of the players and then at himself. He leaves the place, presumably to become lost in Saigon.

In the final scenes of *The Deer Hunter*, Nick is reliving what he could not understand, articulate, or accept. In another backroom, he plays Russian roulette, and he seems to have no identity other than the American who plays roulette. Saigon is burning, and Michael has returned to Vietnam to take Nick back to the states. When Michael finds him, however, and tries to convince him to leave, Nick has no memory of his friend. His face is expressionless, and scars on his arms suggest he has attempted suicide. In a reenactment of their earlier game of roulette, Michael pays to play Nick, in a desperate effort to get through to his friend. In an agonizing few moments of play, Michael escapes the bullet, but Nick loses in this final round of chance. Holding the gun to his temple, just before pulling the trigger, he says, "One shot," echoing Michael's advice for the best, the only, way to get a deer, with one, clean shot. The moment of recognition comes too late for Nick. He pulls the trigger and is gone.

In the character of Nick, loss of identity is a result of the war experience. In *Full Metal Jacket*, loss of individual identity is a goal of military training. Stanley Kubrick's film, based on a novel by Gustav Hasford, tells the story of new marine recruits, first in hellish basic training on Parris Island, South Carolina, and then in combat during the Tet offensive of 1967–1968. Under the brutish regimen of drill instructor Gunnery Sergeant Hartman (Lee Ermey), mostly adolescent young men of all shapes, sizes, religions, and parts of the U.S. are transformed into crisply uniformed, identical marching war machines. For most of the recruits the transformation is not an easy one. For one recruit it is lethal.

The drill instructor's initial words to the recruits capture the theme of basic training: here, he says, "you are all equally worthless." His ceaseless efforts to ridicule and belittle each trainee make them believers. He begins by stripping most of them of their names, giving them new names that personify traits the sergeant finds comical or that make the men appear ridiculous. A Texas recruit becomes "Private Cowboy," and a black recruit is renamed "Private Snowball." Another recruit is nicknamed "Private Joker" because of his propensity for making wisecracks.

One recruit becomes the almost constant target of the sergeant's verbal and physical assaults. Leonard Lawrence (Vincent D'Onofrio), who is overweight, physically weak, and mentally slow, is nicknamed "Private Gomer Pyle." He is ridiculed for his natural demeanor, told to "wipe that disgusting grin" off his face. He is choked and slapped by the instructor. He endures a barrage of punishment and humiliation for his inability to master any of the required tasks and skills. He suffers nobly until the whole platoon turns against him. After uncovering a jelly doughnut in Leonard's unlocked foot locker during inspection, the sergeant takes a different approach to the training of Private Pyle: instead of punishing only Leonard for his infractions and failures, he punishes the entire platoon. One night, tired of the bane Leonard has become in their lives, his fellow trainees gag him, hold him down in his bunk, and beat him until he is sobbing like a child.

The beating works. Leonard becomes a model trainee, even a superb marksman. He is radically changed, however. His face loses any expression, and, at first, he stops speaking. As the sergeant had instructed the recruits, Leonard comes to regard his M14 as an animate being, the only girlfriend he will have while in the Marine Corps. He names his rifle "Charlene" and talks to it. All in all, the drill instructor's training has worked: Leonard can recite regulations on demand, complete the confidence course with the best of the recruits, and look every bit like a polished marine. Drill instructor Hartman has taken the weakest, most pathetic specimen in the platoon and recreated him as a killer. In fact, the last night on the island, before the men ship out for their assignments, Private Leonard Lawrence first shoots the sergeant and then turns the weapon on himself. The poet Wilfred Owen would have appreciated the fact that the shootings occur in the latrine.

Many of these war films show that war and combat can cause mental illness. Many of them also suggest that war is a form of madness, a reality or a perception of reality that contradicts civilian life. In *Apocalypse Now* (1979), Francis Coppola assumes this as his major premise: that war is madness. The setting is the Vietnam War, but Coppola's symbolism and use of archetypes suggest a broader meaning. In the opening sequence Captain Willard (Martin Sheen), United States Army Intelligence, waits in a Saigon hotel room to be assigned his next mission. Imposed over a long shot of a Vietnam jungle as it erupts with bomb fire is a close-up of Willard's head, turned upside down on the screen. The last words of the Doors' hit, "The End," are heard: "All the children are insane." The camera shifts to the hotel room, where Willard's weeklong wait escalates to a drunken anxiety about growing weaker, "softer," the longer he waits. Simply, his will weakens. Through voice-over narration, Willard's point of view is established as the film's perspective. Like a whirling dervish, he practices karate exercises, culminating when he puts his fist through the dresser mirror. He wants to be back in the jungle, he says, but his destruction of the image he sees in the mirror suggests a reluctance, too, to face his shadow self. As the sequence ends, Willard wipes blood from his injured hand onto his face and crouches on the floor, sobbing in anguish.

Willard soon learns that his assignment is to locate one Colonel Walter E. Kurtz, a once celebrated top gun whose ideas and methods have become "unsound." It is 1970 and the U.S. is not militarily posted in Cambodia, yet Kurtz has crossed into Cambodia and is running a rogue operation. In the view of the army, he is evil as well as mad. He has ordered assassinations of high-ranking South Vietnamese military whom his operation has identified as double agents. In describing the situation, the colonel who gives Willard his assignment articulates the basic themes of the movie. In every human heart, he says, there is a conflict between the rational and the irrational, between good and evil, and Kurtz has succumbed to the "temptation to be God." Clearly, only the military high command can do that: hence, Willard's job is to "terminate [Kurtz's] command" and to "terminate with extreme prejudice."

Coppola and John Milius, who coscripted the film, based the characters of Kurtz and Willard and the story itself on Joseph Conrad's *Heart of Darkness*, published in 1902 (Katz 293). In *Heart of Darkness*, Marlow, like Willard in *Apocalypse Now*, is the narrator of the story. Marlow, at the end of the nineteenth century, has a "hankering" (Conrad 2209), he says, to visit Africa, the Congo River, in particular. He manages to get an appointment to pilot a trading boat up the river. In the process of reaching his destination, he hears of and eventually meets Kurtz, the manager of one of the company's trading posts. Kurtz, it seems, has been capable and ambitious, one of the trading company's golden boys. Kurtz's methods, however, have become unsound; they will lose money for his employer. As Marlow travels into the heart of darkness that is the continent, he learns more of Kurtz's fall.

Interestingly, when Marlow is preparing for his trip, he must undergo a physical examination. The company's doctor asks him, "'Ever any madness in your family?'" Marlow is annoyed, perhaps because the doctor has also confided that he is not such a fool as to go "'out there,'" that is, the Congo (2212). The ambiguity of the doctor's matter-of-fact statement that he never sees any of the employees when they return is unsettling also.

In both *Heart of Darkness* and *Apocalypse Now*, madness is established early as a motif. In both stories, too, it is the river symbolically that leads to madness, that psychological break from reality. In *Heart of Darkness* the river is "an immense uncoiled snake" that Marlow says has "charmed" him (2209). Too, there is something timeless and dreamlike about the river:

> Going up that river was like travelling back to the earliest beginnings of the world, when vegetation rioted on the earth and the big trees were kings. . . . you lost your way on that river as you would in a desert, and butted all day long against shoals, trying to find the channel, till you

thought yourself bewitched and cut off for ever from everything you had known once—somewhere—far away—in another existence perhaps. There were moments when one's past came back to one . . . but it came in the shape of an unrestful and noisy dream. (2229)

The river leads one to what Carl Jung later called the shadow, the unconscious self that contains repressed and unexpressed, even primitive and irrational, drives and tendencies. These impulses cannot be categorized simply as evil or destructive. They include positive forces that result, for example, in creativity (Jung 118).

In *Apocalypse Now* a navy patrol boat crew is charged with taking Willard to his destination. As in *Heart of Darkness*, the journey up the river is thematically more important than the destination and what is discovered there. The chaos and dream quality of the journey are foreshadowed by the appearance of Captain Kilgore and his air cavalry. Kilgore, portrayed with gusto by Robert Duvall, and his unit are to escort the patrol boat to the point where it can set in the river.

The sequences involving Kilgore play like a dream, a surrealistic painting where meticulously drawn details dance in slow motion on a billowing canvas. Kilgore, sporting a cavalry hat and yellow neckerchief, leads a worshipful infantry with unflinching command and impeccable military order. The context, the battleground, however, is a bizarre blend of the rational and the irrational. As the helicopters assume attack formation before bombing a Vietnamese village, Kilgore (kill and gore, kill galore) orders the playing of Wagnerian opera. The music, he says, drives the Vietnamese crazy and, thus, is one more weapon in an arsenal designed to destroy not just the physical, but the psyche and the culture of the enemy. On the ground, when some of his men are debating whether to give water to a wounded Vietnamese, Kilgore valiantly orders that his canteen be used for this man who has fought courageously. Kilgore takes the canteen and is about to give water to the man when he is told that one of the patrol boat crew is a well-known surfer from California. A surfing aficionado, Kilgore tosses the canteen to one of his men and dashes off to meet the surfer. In the last scene, as the unit "mops up," Kilgore says to Willard, "I love the smell of napalm in the morning." It "smells like victory," he says, and readers of *Heart of Darkness* are reminded of the ivory which is an ever present reality, the goal of European traders and empire builders who crave it as Kilgore craves victory.

Once the patrol boat is on the river, chaos reigns among the crew. As the eerie stillness and the uncertainty of what surrounds them take hold, military order is superseded by whatever order each individual's personal instincts can provide. For Lance the surfer (Sam Bottoms) order is at first maintained by the familiar rituals of sun worshiping and surfing and later, as the boat gets closer to the jungle, the heart of darkness, by making up his face in camouflage paint to hide from what lies within the jungle. Chef (Frederic Forrest), a saucier from New Orleans, talks of cooking, hunts for mangoes, and becomes hysterical after a face-to-face confrontation with a tiger. The experience is enough to convince him to stay in the boat in the future; the chaos of the river is still safer than the jungle.

The rational and the irrational come into dramatic conflict when the patrol boat encounters a sampan of Vietnamese hauling animals, rice, and other foodstuff. Chef is ordered to board the boat and check out the passengers and cargo. He does so, haphazardly grabbing and spilling the harmless contents in an effort to finish the job and get back on the patrol boat. As a woman lunges toward a basket, one of the American crew opens fire, machine guns blare, and a massacre of the whole boatload of people ensues. A dazed Chef retrieves the hidden cargo the woman was after—a puppy, which Lance, no Arthurian Lancelot, then successfully struggles with Chef to claim as his. When the men see that the woman is still alive, Chef says they must try to get her help. At that point Captain Willard shoots her; his mission, he reminds them, is the priority. Once more in this episode, military protocol has been followed and then supplanted by destructive, shadow instincts.

Like Conrad's Marlow, Willard has said that there is no way of telling Kurtz's story without telling his own. Like Marlow, Willard has "peeped over the edge" (Conrad 2257). In the final sequences, the encounter with Kurtz, viewers see whether Willard is saved, as Marlow is, from stepping over that edge.

The patrol boat reaches the last army outpost before crossing into Cambodia. The outpost is a bridge that is under constant siege. The North Vietnamese destroy it, and the American troops rebuild it so that, as one soldier says, the generals can report the bridge is being held. The scene is a descent into an inferno. Amid flames and smoke in the darkness of night, soldiers wander about—there is no commanding officer;

others hole up in trenches, shell-shocked or, presumably, drunk on alcohol or stoned on drugs; and others lie dead or injured. Willard's earlier comment about Kilgore seems even more apropos now. He wonders what the army "has" on Kurtz. It must be more than insanity and murder since "there was enough of that to go around for everyone."

Willard's question, however, is not answered because Kurtz (Marlon Brando) is a set of contradictions. When the patrol boat approaches his jungle command post, viewers are struck by its quasi-religious appearance. Guarding the embankment are boats of speechless, apparently entranced native people, presumably including some of Kurtz's men. Carved into the mountainside are the ruins of what might have been a temple or another sacred place. The colossal stones conjure up associations not only with the divine but with the Self, which Jung observed (206). Like Conrad's Kurtz, the colonel began as a moral man, a "good" man and a humanitarian, the intelligence officer told Willard. His operation, however, has become a monument to his Self. Within that context any impulse or action is justified.

Again like Conrad's Kurtz, the colonel has engaged in despicable acts—bodies of dead North Vietnamese, Vietcong, and Cambodians are everywhere; some have been beheaded, their heads displayed on the ruin walls, and others have been crucified or hanged. As the captured Willard is led to Kurtz's inner sanctum, he notes the smell of death. In *Heart of Darkness*, the bald head of Kurtz is likened to the ivory that pervades the Europeans' consciousness. In *Apocalypse Now*, Kurtz's baldness suggests Buddha, reinforcing the identification Kurtz has made between himself—his Self—and a deity. Kurtz tells Captain Willard the army has judged him to be a murderer and his methods, unsound; what, he asks, does Willard think of his methods? The captain responds, quite rightly, "I don't see any method at all, sir." Unlike Polonius commenting on Hamlet, Willard sees no thought or design in Kurtz's behavior. Madness, not philosophy or morality, is the issue here.

Kurtz's dying words are "The horror, the horror." They are also the last words of the film, repeated in the narration as Willard leaves the place. In *Heart of Darkness*, Kurtz utters those words as a condemnation not only of the European appetite for dominance but also of his own corruption by that appetite. In *Apocalypse Now*, however, Colonel Kurtz's words are an indictment only of the others, of his superiors and the people in Washington who are running the war. When he reads from T. S. Eliot's poem "The Hollow Men," the recitation is a lament for the misguided others, not for himself.

Like Nick in *The Deer Hunter*, Colonel Kurtz in *Apocalypse Now* has substituted a different reality for the one that, perhaps, he ceased to understand. Likewise, in Philippe DeBroca's classic World War I film satire, *King of Hearts* (1966), the young Scottish soldier who is the story's protagonist chooses to feign madness and join the ranks of the local asylum rather than return to the front. There are numerous ways to read this ending, the most obvious, of course, that life among the insane makes more sense than life among those waging war. Not only is it not sweet or fitting to die for one's country, many of these war films suggest; war is not fitting at all for human beings, patriotic or otherwise.

CHAPTER SEVEN

~

Violence and Mental Illness
A Good Movie Is Hard to Find

In director Samuel Fuller's outrageous melodrama, *Shock Corridor* (1963), violence is a constant in the equation that amounts to mental illness. *Shock Corridor* is the story of an ambitious newspaper reporter who goes undercover as a patient in a mental hospital in order to learn who committed a murder there. Violence is the dominant motif from the start. When John Barrett (Peter Breck) feigns madness to get admitted, he physically attacks a doctor to convince the medical people that he is ill. During the course of the story, the illusion becomes reality as he in fact becomes mentally ill and violent. Violence is also exhibited by other patients; a ward of nymphomaniacs, for example, attack and wound Barrett. The natural violence of 1960s-style shock therapy is made more assaultive since it is administered not as treatment but as punishment for misbehavior. Even the opening and end titles that frame the movie associate madness with violence. The titles use the same quotation from Euripides, the dramatist of ancient Greece: "Whom God wishes to destroy He first makes mad."

The relationship of violence to mental illness is much more complex than Fuller's depiction of it. Before any meaningful discussion of the topic in film can occur, an examination of several important facts about violence and mental illness is warranted. First, in the movies violent behavior is often attributed to mentally ill people, as though the two states are inextricably linked. Second, this association is part of a stereotype of mental illness found throughout American society and particularly throughout the mass media. Third, the available research shows violence to be only moderately linked to mental illness.

Alfred Hitchcock's classic horror film *Psycho* (1960) was one of the first films to achieve both commercial and critical success for exploiting the association of violence with mental illness. The character of Norman Bates, as discussed in chapter 3, wins viewers' sympathy and even empathy at times. In the end, however, the viewer's response is one of terror. The eeriness and wariness surrounding the character reach a climax when Norman and his mother are at last identified as one and the same character, just as the character, the violence, and the mental illness become an inseparable whole. Initially, as Norman describes her to Marion Crane, his mother is "not herself," the utterance insinuating madness. Soon viewers learn that she is murderously ill. At the end, when the mother's personality dominates Norman, he has been devoured by the illness and the mother's rage. Sitting in the police station investigation room, he is no longer Norman. His earlier slight resemblance to his stuffed birds, and his dead mother, is now clearer. No longer Norman, no longer human, the final frames suggest, he is simply insane. That dehumanizing image sums up efficiently the stereotype that occurred in many horror movies.

Twenty years later, in Stanley Kubrick's box office hit *The Shining* (1980), based on the Stephen King horror novel, mental illness is again more fantasy than fact. Jack Torrance (Jack Nicholson) moves with his wife, Wendy (Shelley Duvall), and his son, Danny (Danny Lloyd), to a remote Colorado mountain resort, the Overlook Hotel, where he will serve as the caretaker during the winter months. From November until May the resort is closed because the roads are impassable, and it is occupied only by the caretaker. In the exposition Jack, and viewers, are warned of the danger of the isolation this situation presents, and they are told of an episode several years earlier when the caretaker apparently went insane, murdering his wife and daughters and then killing himself. As viewers easily guess, Jack succumbs to the same cabin fever during his tenure as Overlook overseer.

As played by Nicholson, the character of Jack Torrance becomes one of the most memorable maniacs in American movies. The character is as much fantasy, however, as the spirits that haunt the hotel. Only slight groundwork is laid for Jack's eventual breakdown: several years ago, viewers are told, he dislocated his son's shoulder when he angrily grabbed him in an effort to correct him; he had been drinking during that incident, and he has been a problem drinker, but has sworn off alcohol for five months. These expository details are scant preparation for the rapid transformation Jack undergoes at the Overlook. In little more than a month he regresses from irritability and sleeplessness to abusive language and threatening gestures, and finally to outright violence, as he pursues Wendy and Danny with an axe. For the viewer uninformed about mental illness, the character and the movie clearly reinforce the image of the madman as not only violent but unpredictably and demonically so.

In many other movies that, like *The Shining*, have been box office successes, this image dominates. In Jonathan Demme's *The Silence of the Lambs* (1991), even less foundation is provided than in *The Shining* for the violent behavior of mentally ill characters. "Buffalo Bill" (Ted Levine) is a serial killer that the FBI is pursuing, and Hannibal Lecter (Anthony Hopkins) is the psychiatrist-killer who assists in the search. Both characters are undeniably psychopathic, and their illness is demonstrated in some of the most distasteful, gruesome violence ever captured on film. Hannibal "the Cannibal" murders by attacking and eating his victims, and Buffalo Bill literally skins his female prey. As Otto F. Wahl points out, however, in *Media Madness: Public Images of Mental Illness*, the mentally ill people portrayed in the movies and on television are too often one-dimensional, "characterized primarily, if not exclusively, by the illnesses they suffer" (43). Such is the case with Buffalo Bill and Hannibal Lecter. They are presented almost entirely in terms of their psychopathic, violent behavior; nor is there any meaningful effort to explain the nature, cause, or development of their illness. As Wahl points out, there is a moral corollary, too, in the portrayals. Wahl's comment about media portrayals of mentally ill persons who turn violent applies accurately to both characters in Demme's film: the implication is that "they are tinged with evil. They are more than just criminals. They are morally tainted. They are *bad* people" (75). Since so little of the characters is known, the implication seems accurate.

Even some effective cinematic portrayals of mental illness attribute violent behavior to mentally ill characters. In *Plenty*, Fred Schepisi's faithful rendering of chronic depression, the central character, in one scene unable to control her frustration and anger with a suitor, resorts to firing a pistol and manages to wound him. As volatile as the main character is, her behavior forms part of an organic unity. In *Nuts*, directed by Martin Ritt, the central character's violent behavior is at certain critical moments of the plot both justified and understandable. Unfortunately, such is not always the case in the movies.

The association of violence with mental illness too often mirrors and nurtures a stereotype that pervades society and the media. Many medical and social sciences professionals who have studied the subject of mental illness and violence agree that, in general, people associate dangerous behavior with the mentally ill and that the threat of violence is the major cause of the fear that dominates public response to mental illness (Torrey 56–57; Wahl 71–74). The media promote the stereotype of the mad murderer, as evidenced in the countless newspaper articles, television programs, and movies that feature mentally ill individuals and characters who have killed and injured family members, friends, and total strangers (Torrey 56–57; Wahl 56–65). Says E. Fuller Torrey, M.D.: "Acts of violence by a small number of the mentally ill severely stigmatize all such persons. An association between violent behavior and madness has existed in the mind of the public for hundreds of years; each such publicized incident reinforces this association" (56).

In reality, the relationship of violence to mental illness is not so simple as the stereotype. Reliable studies show that, while some people who have severe mental illnesses are dangerous, most of these people—90 percent—are "neither violent nor dangerous" (Wahl 80).[13] Even researchers who believe that better methods of assessing patients' potential for violence are needed conclude that "the link between mental disorder and violence" is "only modestly greater than chance" (Juss). Only patients who also abuse drugs or alcohol are more likely than people in the general population to behave violently (Juss).

These facts do not deny that some severely mentally ill people are dangerous. Torrey emphasizes this point: "The reality . . . is that there *is* an association between acts of violence and mental illness; insofar as this association continues, it will be difficult to reverse the public stereotype and to decrease discrimination" (57). Torrey presents in comprehensive detail the changes in health care systems and services that are necessary to reduce the incidence of violence among the mentally ill.

Although many movies that depict the mentally ill ignore the basic facts about mental illness and violence, some films have dealt effectively with this complex relationship. Roman Polanski's *Repulsion* (1965) is one. The protagonist, Carol (Catherine Deneuve), is a young, repressed manicurist who shares an apartment in London with her sister. The film tracks Carol's mental deterioration, which culminates in two brutal murders. Neither random nor unpredictable, the character's violent behavior is seen as a natural response of a character whose perception is extremely skewed and who feels severely threatened by men. Polanski masterfully uses black-and-white photography to accent both aspects of the character.

Essential to a sympathetic understanding of Polanski's character is her increasingly bizarre perception. That her perception is central as both a symptom of her mental condition and a harbinger of her later violence is signaled at the start of the film, which is a close-up of an eye, revealed moments later to be that of the protagonist, staring into space, her hands motionless as she gives a manicure at Madame Denise's salon. Early in the film she sees objects and people that aren't there: cracks in the walls, a man in the apartment. She becomes fixated by images and sensations, repetitively brushing something from her face, staring at cracks in the sidewalk pavement. As the story progresses, she hallucinates that she sees huge chasms in the walls, that the walls are soft clay beneath her fingers, that hands emerge like liquid from the walls and grab at her, that she is raped in the apartment.

Carol's violent reaction to these images and sensations is clearly predicted. They are the outward sign of her distorted thoughts about men and sexuality. That her reaction to these perceptions and thoughts will result in violent behavior is foreshadowed several times. Perhaps most telling, she does not want her sister, Helen (Yvonne Furneaux), to go off on vacation with her married lover, thus leaving Carol alone in the apartment for a week. In spite of the repulsion she feels for the lover's "things" being in the bathroom, she not only handles his razor but carries it from the bathroom, using it later to murder the landlord when he tries to seduce her. At the salon a coworker is shocked to find in Carol's purse the severed head of a rabbit, which Helen had planned to cook. Also at the salon Carol cuts a customer's finger, presumably by accident.

In *Repulsion*, Polanski carefully lays the groundwork for the character's violent murders. Even in black-and-white, they are brutal, as Carol hits her first victim, a potential and persistent beau, repeatedly with a candlestick and later slashes the landlord repeatedly with the razor. These acts are not random or unpredictable, however, as such violence is so often portrayed in movies about people who are mentally disturbed. At the movie's end viewers are reminded that there is something about the way Carol sees and perceives that separates her. The character now in a catatonic state, the camera moves to a close-up of the family photo. The focus narrows to the little girl in the picture who is Carol, who looks away from the photographer into the distance, and then to her eyes, ending as the film began, with a close-up of one eye staring vacantly.

In strong contrast to *Repulsion* is the more recent *Girl, Interrupted* (1999), also a movie about a young woman, Susanna Kaysen (Winona Ryder), who is mentally ill. The story takes place in the late 1960s in a Boston-area psychiatric hospital known for its excellent, progressive treatment and its well-to-do patients, including poets, songwriters, and other artists. Directed by James Mangold and based loosely on Kaysen's memoir of the same title, *Girl, Interrupted* is more powerful in the threat of violent behavior it communicates than in the actual violence it depicts. In contrast to *Repulsion*, again, *Girl, Interrupted* accents the violence that people with severe mental illnesses sometimes do to themselves rather than to others. Severely mentally ill persons are, in fact, "far more likely" to hurt themselves than others, according to one medical study (Ferriman).

Like Polanski's film, *Girl, Interrupted* emphasizes the difficulties in perception and thinking that often characterize someone who has a severe mental illness, in Susanna's case borderline personality disorder. The point of view is clearly established in the opening, as the voice of the central character asks, "Have you ever confused a dream with life? Or stolen something when you have the cash? Have you ever been blue or thought your train moving while sitting still? Maybe I *was* just crazy. Maybe it was the sixties. Or maybe I was just a girl, interrupted." Susanna's fluctuating self-image, moods, and attitudes toward others are manifested in feelings of boredom and depression and in self-mutilation (bruising her wrists) and suicide attempts.

Susanna is one of several patients in her ward who have a history of physically hurting themselves. One young woman, whose face, arm, and hand are severely scarred, poured gasoline on herself and lit a match when she was ten years old. Another patient is anorexically thin at seventy-some pounds. Still another, whose father has her discharged, hangs herself shortly after being moved into her own apartment. Lisa (Angelina Jolie), the most compelling character in the film, abuses drugs and threatens suicide. Interestingly, Susanna is incredulous, in spite of her history, when she is not allowed to shave her legs in private. Her response reflects the lack of insight, or understanding of her disease, that is often a problem in the treatment of serious mental illness.

Only Lisa seems to present a physical threat to others. Lean and quick in her movements, she has a feline stealthiness about her. More than self-assured, aggressive, in her manner and language, she intimidates patients and staff alike. Only Valerie (Whoopi Goldberg), the supervising nurse on the ward, refuses to back down when Lisa approaches or confronts her. When manic, Lisa resists the staff's efforts to control her, and must be physically restrained and secluded. Only once does she actually strike someone, a patient, but the force of the assault is hard and loud. At the end of the film, when she is medicated and restrained, her aggressiveness is shown to be exactly what it is, a veneer that conceals severe and debilitating illness.

Something of a companion piece to *Repulsion* is Martin Scorsese's *Taxi Driver* (1976), a depiction of the repressed male. The film remains controversial for its violence and point of view (Magill's). *Taxi Driver*, however, must be applauded for its intense and realistic character portrayal and for the careful link it makes between mental illness and violence. Travis Bickle (Robert De Niro), the protagonist and dominating consciousness of the film, is no random murderer, but a disturbed mind who carefully conceives and executes a plan that he believes will help cleanse the world of its hypocrisy and immorality.

Travis Bickle is a twenty-six-year-old ex-marine—he was honorably discharged several years earlier—living in New York City who has trouble sleeping and, in an effort to do something with all those sleepless hours, gets a job driving a taxi at night. Besides insomnia, he suffers from headaches and consumes steady doses of aspirin, he is wracked by indigestion—he comes to believe he has stomach cancer—and keeps a multitude of medicine bottles next to his bed, he lives on a diet of junk food and sugar, and he drinks periodically from a pint bottle of liquor he keeps in the military field jacket he wears. He is obsessed with the material and nonmaterial filth he sees throughout the city: trash in the streets, and garbage in the hearts of the people who pimp, prostitute, steal, and assault one another in sundry ways. By the film's climax, when Travis goes on his bloody shooting spree, the dark circles around his eyes give his face an eerie skeletal appearance.

Travis Bickle shows symptoms of a severe mental illness, although its nature or cause is not clear. It resembles posttraumatic stress disorder as well as borderline personality disorder and bipolar disease. What is clear are the symptoms: his obsessiveness, his distorted perceptions of the city and its people, his repressed sexuality, and, finally, his psychotic behavior. As might be expected of such a character, he is not consistent in his thoughts or behavior. Betsy (Cybill Shepherd), the political campaign volunteer with whom he becomes obsessed, rightly describes him as a set of "contradictions." On one hand, he is extremely polite in his speech and manners; on the other, he takes Betsy to a pornographic movie and does not understand why she is offended. He constantly rails about the city's crime, drugs, and prostitution, but he spends many of his free hours in adult-movie theaters. Travis Bickle tends to see the world in stark absolutes: right and wrong, good and evil, pure and impure. When Betsy, whom he has idealized for her purity and beauty, rejects him, she joins the ranks of the "cold and distant," the lying, hypocritical masses that make up the city.

Travis's violent behavior is predicted. In his narrative and his remarks to others, he is fixated on the idea of the city's filth. He also warns that he is reaching a breaking point. He tells a fellow cabbie whom he seems to respect that he is depressed, that "things" have him "down." He tells the Wizard (Peter Boyle) that he wants to "go out and really do something," that he has "some bad ideas" in his head. One psychiatrist's observation about anger applies well to Travis: "The perception of unfairness or injustice is the ultimate cause of most, if not all, anger" (Burns 145). In response to his perceptions and conclusions that the world operates from a base of injustice, he prepares to do battle. He goes into training, exercising and giving up pills and bad food, illegally purchases an arsenal of guns and ammunition, and finally dresses, like a knight of old, for combat. He thinks of himself as "a man who will not take it anymore."

In his final transformation to soldier/vigilante/terrorist, Travis resembles Private Leonard Lawrence in *Full Metal Jacket*, another soldier who, unable to take it anymore, is reduced to the thing he cannot understand and hates. Travis becomes an instrument of the injustice he cannot understand and abhors. In the violent climax of the film, Travis unleashes his rage against those who victimize Iris (Jodie Foster), a twelve-year-old prostitute that Travis befriends. An earlier attempt to assassinate Betsy's presidential candidate was thwarted by the Secret Service. The point, however, is not the particular target of Travis's rage but the rage itself. Each of the targets is known to some degree, and each is perceived to be an instrument of hypocrisy and injustice.

Scorsese should have ended *Taxi Driver* with Travis's shooting rampage and death. Unfortunately, Travis survives, and the film transforms him into a hero. Contrary to all the evidence that he is seriously disturbed, New York City officials laud his actions, and at the end of the story he is again working as a cabbie. An otherwise powerful portrayal of violence and mental illness is marred by this comic lapse into fantasy.

A unified, flawless portrayal of violence in someone who is mentally ill is found in Scorsese's *Raging Bull* (1980), the story of 1940s middleweight boxing champion Jake La Motta (Robert De Niro). Based on La Motta's ghostwritten biography, the screenplay was written by longtime Scorsese associates Paul Schrader and Mardik Martin. Like *Taxi Driver*, also written by Schrader, and *Affliction*, directed by Schrader, *Raging Bull* paints a vivid portrait of a man who is mentally and emotionally unbalanced and whose rage becomes his signature trait. Less concerned with La Motta the boxer than with La Motta the man, *Raging Bull* presents the fighter's boxing career as only one part of a life lived violently.

The film covers the years 1941–1964, tracking La Motta's boxing career from the early years, when he first made a name for himself, to

1949, when he won the middleweight championship, to 1951, when he lost the title in a savage bout with Sugar Ray Robinson, and finally to 1956, when he retired to open a nightclub. In tandem with La Motta's fight career, the film shows his disastrous personal life, chronicling his tempestuous marriages and relationship with his brother, Joey (Joe Pesci). In all of this story violence is the tone and the substance, and even though it was shot primarily in black-and-white it is possibly the bloodiest, most violent film ever made. Even in its sound track *Raging Bull* assaults the viewer, in the boxing ring with the thuds and cracks of gloves pounding and ripping flesh, and in domestic battles with husbands and wives thundering and screaming at each other, and furniture being overturned and driven to the ground.

The primary source of the violence in this chronicle is the protagonist. From the start he is an explosive, stubborn personality. Born and raised in the Bronx, he wants to escape it, but on his own terms. As a result, he has an uncanny way of antagonizing anyone who might help him. The story reveals little about his childhood and therefore no insight into what might have produced such a personality. His father's apartment is filled with crucifixes, statues, and other objects of Catholic devotion. There and in Jake's own home, a crucifix hangs above the headboard in the bedroom. His and his brother's attitude toward women also suggests a rigid, patriarchal upbringing. Whatever the cause, La Motta is disturbed, and his condition worsens with the years. His marriage to his second wife, Vickie (Cathy Moriarty), and his relationship with Joey are both devastated by his jealousy and paranoia. His suspicions that Vickie has been unfaithful to him culminate in his delusion that she has had an affair with Joey.

As unlikable as Jake La Motta is, he is also a character with whom viewers sympathize. Possessed of limited intelligence and scarce self-knowledge, he frequently is a hostage of his distorted perceptions, and of his jealousy, paranoia, and anger. In addition, if he needs to punish Vickie and Joey for what he sees as their transgressions, he also seems to need to be punished. Perhaps the most poignant dramatization of these tragic flaws occurs toward the end of the film, in a sequence showing him being jailed after an arrest on a vice charge resulting from a fourteen-year-old girl being served in his nightclub. After violently resisting his jailers, he is hurled into the cell. Moments later, he begins to pound his head against the concrete wall, crying out that he is stupid and asking, "Why?" He wants to know both why he could behave so stupidly and why he should be treated this way—he's "not that bad." Why didn't someone stop him or help him, he wants to know.

Scorsese uses slow motion photography to underscore the film's concern with perception. In a number of the fight scenes, use of slow motion accents the boxer's distorted perception after being brutally punched and pummeled. Slow motion also highlights Jake's problems with perception and his inability to control or overcome what he is. In the opening, as the credits roll, a lone boxer, robed and hooded, warms up in the ring in slow motion. Soothing tones from Mascagni's opera *Cavalleria Rusticana* play, transforming the boxer's exercise into the flowing movement of a balletic dance. Quickly viewers see that this dreamlike image is in stark contrast to the reality of the raging bull, "the Bronx bull."

In another dreamlike scene slow motion emphasizes Jake's need to "win" Vickie, a beautiful blonde and 1940s movie star look-alike. Even though he is married, he has seen her at a Bronx swimming pool and has determined that he wants her. In this scene he watches her from across a dance room. In slow motion Salvy, a small-time hood who is often in her company and who, Jake complains, thinks he's a "big shot," approaches her table, and they leave the dance as Jake follows them from the building. Underlying Jake's need to romance and acquire Vickie is a need to feel self-worth. Earlier, he obsesses in a conversation with Joey about having small hands: his size will disqualify him from ever fighting the best, heavyweights such as Joe Lewis. Since his hands, to a great extent, determine his ranking and value in the world, it may not be an exaggeration to say that he is lamenting his deficient ego. Vickie is the trophy that verifies his worth, maybe even his manliness.

Much later in the film another use of slow motion underscores Jake's estrangement from his brother and suggests his awareness of the price of that loss. The year is 1958, Jake has retired from the ring and served jail time, and now he works in a sleazy bar. He and Joey have been estranged for years, ever since Jake accused him of having an affair with Vickie and then beat him in front of his wife and children. One night in 1958, as Jake gets a taxi for a girlfriend, he sees Joey entering a grocery. The motion slows as Joey approaches the door, opens it, and enters the shop. When he exits, Jake tries to reconcile with him but is unsuccessful. In fact, his display of affection embarrasses and disgusts Joey.

In *Affliction* the protagonist shares some of the symptoms and behavior of the angry young men of *Taxi Driver* and *Raging Bull*. Adapted by director Schrader from Russell Banks's novel, *Affliction* adds an important dimension to the portrayal of male anger in linking the character's behavior to the abuse he suffered as a child at the hands of his father. The story takes place in early winter during deer hunting season in and around the small town of Lawford in upstate New Hampshire. Wade Whitehouse (Nick Nolte) is Lawford's only police officer; he also does various odd jobs, which include running the snow plow and serving as crossing guard at the local elementary school. Well-intentioned, Wade nonetheless is the town ne'er-do-well, with a history of being feisty, drinking too much, and sometimes turning violent.

A hunting accident is the catalyst, but not the cause, for Whitehouse's final and complete deterioration. When a high-ranking official from Massachusetts, an acquaintance of one of the local selectmen, accidentally shoots and kills himself, Wade becomes convinced that his friend, who had been hired to accompany the hunter, was paid to kill the man. Wade weaves a conspiracy theory that implicates several local businessmen as well as the mafia. As his paranoia grows, it engulfs his life. Gnawing suspicions that his ex-wife is "out to get him" motivate him to begin a child custody battle. As these suspicions grow, he becomes increasingly frustrated at his inability to resolve any of his problems, he loses the little trust he has for those who try to befriend him, and he turns frighteningly violent, even toward his young daughter.

The most important factor in Wade's history is his father. In fact, the cause of his paranoia and frustration is, to a great extent, his anger toward his father, a coarse, alcoholic, abusive tyrant played magnificently by James Coburn. Flashbacks tie this traumatic relationship to the current events of Wade's life. As he plays traffic cop at the school, his arms outstretched in a crucified-Christ pose, he stares trancelike into space, remembering his daughter saying she loves him but doesn't want to stay with him in Lawford. His sense of inadequacy deepens. As he talks to his girlfriend, Marge (Sissy Spacek), about his failed marriage, a flashback reveals his father ridiculing and hitting him as an adolescent, throwing him to the floor.

When Wade's mother dies, the convergence of past and present enters real time. One exceptionally cold morning, he and Marge drive out to his parents' farm and discover that his mother is dead. The house is unheated because Wade's father failed to get the furnace fixed. He did not feel the cold because of his alcohol consumption, but she died in her sleep from the cold. Now Wade's father again becomes a part of his life, as the family members gather for the funeral and as Wade and Marge move to the farm to supervise Glen Whitehouse.

A couple of times during the story Wade refers to himself as a whipped dog. The image of defeat, like the early suggestions of his propensity to violence, foreshadow his outcome. From the onset he is plagued by a toothache and complains of the pain to everyone he encounters. As his paranoia and his anger about other events grow, so too does his dental pain. Late in the story he finally attempts to make an appointment with a dentist, but he cannot get one right away. In his frustration he extracts the tooth himself using pliers. Although the toothache might be considered symbolic of the emotional illness that afflicts him, when he eliminates the tooth he is still hounded by his out-of-control emotions. There seems to be no escaping his affliction. In one scene he looks in the mirror but tells his brother he sees only a stranger. Perhaps that stranger is no stranger at all, but his father, the man he is becoming. Even at the end, when Wade kills and then sets fire to Glen, there is no escape. This is not a purgative fire. Still convinced that his friend killed the hunter, he hunts down his friend and kills him.

Violence is everywhere in twenty-first century America, including the movies. It should come as no surprise that violence abounds in films that portray people with mental illness since the association of violence with mental illness remains strong. Continuing research shows that some severely mentally ill persons do commit acts of violence, but no research indicates that violence is a necessary symptom or manifestation of mental illness. Filmgoers should expect that movies depict the relationship of violence and mental illness both believably and congruously.

~

Notes

1. Several writers have discussed the exploitation of mental illness in the movies through the use of stereotypes. In addition to Otto Wahl, *Media Madness: Public Images of Mental Illness*, see Michael Fleming and Roger Manvell, *Images of Madness: The Portrayal of Insanity in the Feature Film*, Rutherford, N.J.: Fairleigh Dickinson University Press, 1985. For a description of movie stereotypes of the psychiatrist, see Irving Schneider, M.D., "The Theory and Practice of Movie Psychiatry."

2. See particularly chapter 6, "The False-Self System."

3. Indeed, the character exhibits several characteristics described in the American Psychiatric Association's *Diagnostic and Statistical Manual of Mental Disorders*, for example, fear of rejection and abandonment, which can lead to changes in self-image and behavior (706).

4. As Donald Spoto points out, both of these techniques, involving light-shadow and interior-exterior, are typical of Hitchcock. Spoto discusses their frequent occurrence in the director's works, including *Rebecca*, *Vertigo*, and *Psycho* (92, 300, 364).

5. Appearances versus reality, too, is a recurring theme in Hitchcock's work. Spoto comments on it in relation to several films, including *Spellbound* and *The Man Who Knew Too Much* (155, 273). The topic is particularly pertinent to Hitchcock's treatment of mental illness.

6. Chaos inflicted from the outside world is a frequent motif in Hitchcock's movies, as Donald Spoto notes in *Shadow of a Doubt* (137–138), *The Man Who*

Knew Too Much (269), *The Wrong Man* (285), *Vertigo* (323), *Psycho* (362–365, 370), *The Birds* (385–386), and *Marnie* (404). Often the chaos inflicted on characters, Spoto observes, is preceded and accompanied by the characters' restlessness or sense of boredom.

7. The following articles are among studies that explore this relationship: Krystine Irene Batcho, "Nostalgia: A Psychological Perspective," *Perceptual and Motor Skills* 80 (1995): 131–143; and Rhonda G. Parker, "Reminiscence: A Continuity Theory Framework," *Gerontologist* 35 (August 1995): 515–525, FirstSearch, 29 March 2001.

8. Hyler summarizes the diagnostic criteria for borderline personality disorder (BPD), as described in the fourth edition of the *Diagnostic and Statistical Manual of Mental Disorders*, and notes examples of these behaviors in major feature films. Among the films he includes are *Play Misty for Me* (1971), *Fatal Attraction* (1987), *Misery* (1990), *Looking for Mr. Goodbar* (1977), *Frances* (1982), and *Raging Bull* (1980).

9. Gutin notes especially the research and writings of Kay Redfield Jamison and Arnold Ludwig.

10. According to the *Diagnostic and Statistical Manual of Mental Disorders*, the hallucinations associated with schizophrenia are most often auditory (299–300).

11. The literature possibly would include descriptions of conversion disorders. In the *Diagnostic and Statistical Manual of Mental Disorders*, symptoms of such disorders can include paralysis of a limb, difficulty swallowing, and other motor and sensory dysfunction (492–493). The phenomenon of stigmata does not appear to be completely understood within the medical community. In the *Psychiatric Dictionary*, 3d ed. (New York: Oxford University Press, 1960), Leland E. Hinsie, M.D., and Robert Jean Campbell, M.D., assert: "Most psychoanalytic writers would consider these monosymptomatic conversions, the afflicted areas unconsciously symbolizing the genitals" (696). Dr. Livingston in *Agnes of God* may also have in mind self-mutilation that can accompany borderline personality disorder.

12. Numerous versions of the legend exist. The details here rely on *Bulfinch's Mythology*.

13. See also Carter 229 and U.S. Dept. of Health and Human Services. *Mental Health: A Report of the Surgeon General.*

~

Sources Cited

Abrams, M. H., ed. *The Norton Anthology of English Literature.* 2 vols. 6th ed. New York: W. W. Norton, 1993.

———. *The Norton Anthology of English Literature: The Major Authors.* 6th ed. New York: W. W. Norton, 1996.

American Psychiatric Association. *Diagnostic and Statistical Manual of Mental Disorders.* 4th ed. Text Revision. Washington, D.C.: American Psychiatric Association, 2000.

Blake, William. "The Book of Thel." In David Perkins, ed., *English Romantic Writers* (New York: Harcourt, Brace, 1967), 65–68.

———. "The Marriage of Heaven and Hell." In David Perkins, ed., *English Romantic Writers* (New York: Harcourt, Brace, 1967), 68–75.

Bulfinch, Thomas. *Bulfinch's Mythology.* New York: Avenel, 1979.

Burns, David D. *Feeling Good: The New Mood Therapy.* New York: New American Library, 1980.

Carter, Rosalynn. *Helping Someone with Mental Illness: A Compassionate Guide for Family, Friends, and Caregivers.* With Susan K. Golant. New York: Random House, 1998.

Conrad, Joseph. *Heart of Darkness.* In M. H. Abrams, *The Norton Anthology of English Literature: The Major Authors,* 6th ed. (New York: W. W. Norton, 1996), 2205–2263.

Ferriman, Annabel. "The Stigma of Schizophrenia." *British Medical Journal,* February 19, 2000. Accessed in Periodical Abstracts, Jan. 22, 2001.

Foucault, Michel. *Madness and Civilization: A History of Insanity in the Age of Reason.* Translated by Richard Howard. New York: Random House, 1965.

Gettings, Fred. *Dictionary of Demons: A Guide to Demons and Demonologists in Occult Lore.* North Pomfret, Vt.: Trafalgar Square, 1988.

Gutin, Jo Ann C. "That Fine Madness." *Discover* 17 (1996). Accessed in Periodical Abstracts, Nov. 5, 1999.

Halliwell, Leslie. *Halliwell's Film Guide.* 7th ed. New York: Harper & Row, 1989.

Hudgens, Richard. Professor of Psychiatry, Washington University in St. Louis School of Medicine. Interview by author, July 22, 2002.

Hyler, Steven E. "Using Commercially Available Films to Teach about Borderline Personality Disorder." *Bulletin of the Menninger Clinic* 61 (1997). Accessed in Academic Search Elite, March 27, 2000.

James, William. *The Varieties of Religious Experience.* Lectures delivered in 1901–1902. Garden City, N.Y.: Doubleday, 1978.

Jones, Anne Hudson. "Literature and Medicine: Narratives of Mental Illness." *Lancet* 350 (1997): 359–361. Accessed in Periodical Abstracts, May 13, 1999.

Jung, Carl G. *Man and His Symbols.* New York: Doubleday, 1964.

Juss, Satvinder. "Modest Link between Mental Illness and Violence." *Lancet* 34 (1997). Accessed in Periodical Abstracts, Dec. 3, 1999.

Katz, Ephraim. *The Film Encyclopedia.* 3d ed. Revised by Fred Klein and Ronald Dean Nolan. New York: HarperCollins, 1998.

Keats, John. "The Eve of St. Agnes." In David Perkins, ed., *English Romantic Writers* (New York: Harcourt, Brace, 1967), 1173–1179.

Laing, R. D. *The Divided Self.* New York: Random House, 1960.

Ludwig, Arnold M. "Mental Disturbance and Creative Achievement." *Harvard Mental Health Letter* 12 (1996). Accessed in the Health Reference Center, Oct. 27, 1999.

Maltin, Leonard, ed. *Movie and Video Guide.* 2001 ed. New York: New American Library, 2000.

Milstone, Carol. "Sybil Minds." *Saturday Night,* September 1997, 35–42. Accessed in Periodical Abstracts, Feb. 25, 1999.

Napoli, Mary. "A Beautiful Mind: Movie Misrepresents the Recovery of John F. Nash Jr." *Healthfacts,* April 2002, 3. Accessed in Periodical Abstracts, March 10, 2003.

Owen, Wilfred. "Dulce Et Decorum Est." In M. H. Abrams, ed., *The Norton Anthology of English Literature,* 6th ed. (New York: W. W. Norton, 1993), 2:1845–1846.

Perkins, David, ed. *English Romantic Writers*. New York: Harcourt, Brace, 1967.

Perry, Dennis R. "Imps of the Perverse: Discovering the Poe/Hitchcock Connection." *Literature Film Quarterly* 24 (1996). Accessed in Academic Search Elite, March 24, 2000.

Rosen, George. *Madness in Society: Chapters in the Historical Sociology of Mental Illness*. Chicago: University of Chicago Press, 1968.

Schneider, Irving. "The Theory and Practice of Movie Psychiatry." *American Journal of Psychiatry* 144 (1987): 996–1002.

Shakespeare, William. *The Tragedy of Hamlet, Prince of Denmark*. Edited by William Farnham. Baltimore, Md.: Penguin, 1957.

Spoto, Donald. *The Art of Alfred Hitchcock: Fifty Years of His Motion Pictures*. New York: Hopkinson & Blake, 1976.

Styron, William. *Darkness Visible: A Memoir of Madness*. New York: Random House, 1990.

"Taxi Driver." *Magill's Survey of Cinema*, June 15, 1995. Accessed in Electric Library, May 11, 2001.

Tennyson, Alfred, Lord. "Ulysses." In M. H. Abrams, *The Norton Anthology of English Literature: The Major Authors*, 6th ed. (New York: W. W. Norton, 1996), 1891–1893.

Torrey, E. Fuller. *Out of the Shadows: Confronting America's Mental Illness Crisis*. New York: John Wiley, 1997.

Truffaut, Francois. *Hitchcock*. With Helen G. Scott. New York: Simon & Schuster, 1966.

U.S. Dept. of Health and Human Services. *Mental Health: A Report of the Surgeon General*. Rockville, Md.: U.S. Dept. of Health and Human Services, Substance Abuse and Mental Health Services Administration, Center for Mental Health Services, National Institutes of Health, National Institute of Mental Health, 1999.

Wahl, Otto F. *Media Madness: Public Images of Mental Illness*. New Brunswick, N.J.: Rutgers University Press, 1995.

Films Discussed and/or Cited

Affliction. Dir. Paul Schrader. Wr. Paul Schrader. Based on the novel by Russell Banks. Largo Entertainment, 1997.

Agnes of God. Dir. Norman Jewison. Scr. John Pielmeier. From a play by Pielmeier. Columbia Pictures, 1985.

An Angel at My Table. Dir. Jane Campion. Scr. Laura Jones. Based on the autobiographies of Janet Frame. New Line Cinema, 1989.

Apocalypse Now. Dir. Francis Ford Coppola. Wr. John Milius and Coppola. 1979.

As Good As It Gets. Dir. James L. Brooks. Scr. Mark Andrus and James L. Brooks. Story by Mark Andrus. TriStar Pictures, 1997.

A Beautiful Mind. Dir. Ron Howard. Wr. Akiva Goldsman. Based on the book by Sylvia Nasar. Universal Studios, 2001.

Beloved. Dir. Jonathan Demme. Scr. Akosua Busia, Richard LaGravenese, and Adam Brooks. Based on the novel by Toni Morrison. Touchstone Pictures, 1998.

Benny & Joon. Dir. Jeremiah Chechik. Scr. Barry Berman. Story by Barry Berman and Leslie McNeil. 1993.

The Best Years of Our Lives. Dir. William Wyler. Scr. Robert E. Sherwood. From a novel by MacKinlay Kantor. 1946. Videocassette. MGM Home Entertainment, 2000.

The Birds. Dir. Alfred Hitchcock. Scr. Evan Hunter. Based on a story by Daphne du Maurier. Alfred Hitchcock Productions, 1963.

Born on the Fourth of July. Dir. Oliver Stone. Scr. Oliver Stone and Ron Kovic. Based on the book by Ron Kovic. 1989.

The Caine Mutiny. Dir. Edward Dmytryk. Scr. Stanley Roberts. Additional dialogue by Michael Blankfort. Based on the novel by Herman Wouk. 1954. Videocassette. Columbia TriStar Home Video, 1992.

Captain Newman, M.D. Dir. David Miller. Scr. Richard L. Breen, Phoebe and Henry Ephron. From the novel by Leo Rosten. 1963. Videocassette. MCA Home Video, 1987.

The Caretakers. Dir. Hall Bartlett. Scr. Henry F. Greenberg. Screen story by Hall Bartlett and Jerry Paris. Based on the book by Dariel Telfer. 1963. Videocassette. MGM/UA Home Video, 1996.

Chattahoochee. Dir. Mick Jackson. Wr. James Hicks. Hemdale Film Corp., 1990.

Coming Home. Dir. Hal Ashby. Scr. Waldo Salt and Robert C. Jones. Story by Nancy Dowd. Metro-Goldwyn-Mayer, 1978.

Cross Creek. Dir. Martin Ritt. Scr. Dalene Young. Based on Marjorie Kinnan Rawlings's memoirs *Cross Creek*. 1983.

David and Lisa. Dir. Frank Perry. Scr. Eleanor Perry. Based on a book by Theodore Isaac Rubin, M.D. 1962. Videocassette. Fox Lorber Home Video, 1990.

Dead Poets Society. Dir. Peter Weir. Wr. Tom Schulman. 1989.

The Deer Hunter. Dir. Michael Cimino. Scr. Deric Washburn. Story by Michael Cimino, Deric Washburn, Louis Garfinkle, and Quinn K. Redeker. EMI Films, 1978.

Don't Bother to Knock. Dir. Roy Baker. Wr. Daniel Taradash. From a novel by Charlotte Armstrong. 1952. Videocassette.

Equus. Dir. Sidney Lumet. Scr. Peter Shaffer. From a play by Shaffer. 1977. Videocassette.

Fatal Attraction. Dir. Adrian Lyne. Scr. James Dearden. 1987.

Fear Strikes Out. Dir. Robert Mulligan. Scr. Ted Berkman and Raphael Blau. Based on a story by James A. Piersall and Albert S. Hirshberg. 1956. Videocassette. Paramount Pictures, 1990.

Finding Forrester. Dir. Gus Van Sant. Wr. Mike Rich. 2001.

A Fine Madness. Dir. Irvin Kershner. Scr. Elliott Baker. 1966. Videocassette. Warner Home Video, 1991.

The Fisher King. Dir. Terry Gilliam. Wr. Richard LaGravenese. TriStar Pictures, 1991.

Frances. Dir. Graeme Clifford. Wr. Eric Bergren, Christopher DeVore, and Nicholas Kazan. EMI Films, 1982.

Full Metal Jacket. Dir. Stanley Kubrick. Scr. Stanley Kubrick, Michael Kerr, and Gustav Hasford. Adapted from *The Short-Timers* by Hasford. Warner Bros., 1987.

Girl, Interrupted. Dir. James Mangold. Scr. James Mangold, Lisa Loomer, and Anna Hamilton Phelan. Based on the book by Susanna Kaysen. Columbia Pictures, 1999.

Good Will Hunting. Dir. Gus Van Sant. Wr. Ben Affleck and Matt Damon. Miramax Films, 1997.

Hush . . . Hush, Sweet Charlotte. Dir. Robert Aldrich. 1964.

King of Hearts. Dir. Philippe De Broca. Scr. Daniel Boulanger. 1966. Videocassette. MGM/UA Home Video, 1990.

Lilith. Dir. Robert Rossen. Scr. Robert Rossen. Based on the novel by J. R. Salamanca. 1964. Videocassette.

Losing Chase. Dir. Kevin Bacon. Wr. Anne Meredith. 1996. Videocassette.

The Madness of King George. Dir. Nicholas Hytner. Adapted by Alan Bennett. From a play by Alan Bennett. 1994.

The Man in the Gray Flannel Suit. Dir. Nunnally Johnson. Wr. Nunnally Johnson. From the novel by Sloan Wilson. 1956. Videocassette. Twentieth Century Fox Home Entertainment, 1997.

The Man Who Knew Too Much. Dir. Alfred Hitchcock. Scr. John Michael Hayes. Based on a story by Charles Bennett and D. B. Wyndham-Lewis. 1955. Videocassette. Universal Studios, 1999.

Marnie. Dir. Alfred Hitchcock. Scr. Jay Presson Allen. From the novel by Winston Graham. Geoffrey Stanley, Inc., 1964.

Now, Voyager. Dir. Irving Rapper. Scr. Casey Robinson. From the novel by Olive Higgins Prouty. 1942. Videocassette. MGM Home Entertainment, 1997.

Nuts. Dir. Martin Ritt. Scr. Tom Topor, Darryl Ponicsan, and Alvin Sargent. Based on a play by Topor. 1987.

One Flew over the Cuckoo's Nest. Dir. Milos Forman. Wr. Lawrence Hauben and Bo Goldman. From a novel by Ken Kesey. 1975.

Ordinary People. Dir. Robert Redford. Scr. Alvin Sargent. From the novel by Judith Guest. 1980.

Platoon. Dir. Oliver Stone. Wr. Oliver Stone. 1986.

Play Misty for Me. Dir. Clint Eastwood. Scr. Jo Heims and Dean Riesner. Story by Jo Heims. Universal Pictures and the Malpaso Company, 1971.

Plenty. Dir. Fred Schepisi. Scr. David Hare. Based on the play by David Hare. Edward R. Pressman Film Corporation and RKO Pictures, 1985.

Possessed. Dir. Curtis Bernhardt. Scr. Sylvia Richards and Ranald MacDougall. Based on a story by Rita Weiman. 1947. Videocassette. MGM/UA Home Video and Turner Entertainment, 1991.

Psycho. Dir. Alfred Hitchcock. Scr. Joseph Stefano. Based on the novel by Robert Bloch. Shamley Productions, 1960.

Raging Bull. Dir. Martin Scorsese. Scr. Paul Schrader and Mardik Martin. Based on the book by Jake LaMotta with Joseph Carter and Peter Savage. Metro-Goldwyn-Mayer, 1980.

The Rain People. Dir. Francis Ford Coppola. Wr. Coppola. 1969. Videocassette. Warner Home Video, 1993.

Raintree County. Dir. Edward Dmytryk. Scr. Millard Kaufman. Based on the novel by Ross Lockridge Jr. 1957. Videocassette.

Rebecca. Dir. Alfred Hitchcock. Scr. Robert E. Sherwood and Joan Harrison. Based on the novel by Daphne du Maurier. 1940. Videocassette. Anchor Bay Entertainment, 1998.

Repulsion. Dir. Roman Polanski. Scr. Polanski and Gerard Brach. Columbia Pictures, 1965.

Saving Private Ryan. Dir. Steven Spielberg. Wr. Robert Rodat. 1998.

Scent of a Woman. Dir. Martin Brest. Scr. Bo Goldman. Based on Italian film *Profumo di Donna.* 1992.

Shadow of a Doubt. Dir. Alfred Hitchcock. Scr. Thornton Wilder, Sally Benson, and Alma Reville. From a story by Gordon McDonell. 1942. Videocassette. Universal Studios, 1999.

Shine. Dir. Scott Hicks. Scr. Jan Sardi. From a story by Scott Hicks. 1996.

The Shining. Dir. Stanley Kubrick. Scr. Kubrick and Diane Johnson. Based on the novel by Stephen King. Warner Bros., 1980.

Shock Corridor. Dir. Samuel Fuller. Wr. Fuller. F & F Productions, 1963.

The Silence of the Lambs. Dir. Jonathan Demme. Scr. Ted Tally. Based on the novel by Thomas Harris. Orion Pictures, 1991.

The Snake Pit. Dir. Anatole Litvak. Scr. Frank Partos and Millen Brand. Based on the novel by Mary Jane Ward. 1948. Videocassette. Fox Video, 1993.

Sophie's Choice. Dir. Alan J. Pakula. Scr. Pakula. Based on the novel by William Styron. ITC Films, 1982.

Spellbound. Dir. Alfred Hitchcock. Scr. Ben Hecht. 1945. Videocassette. CBS/Fox, 1996.

Splendor in the Grass. Dir. Elia Kazan. Wr. William Inge. Warner Bros., 1961.

A Streetcar Named Desire. Dir. Elia Kazan. Scr. Tennessee Williams. From a play by Williams. 1951. Videocassette.

Suddenly, Last Summer. Dir. Joseph Mankiewicz. Wr. Gore Vidal and Tennesee Williams. Based on the play by Tennessee Williams. 1959. Videocassette. Columbia TriStar, 1986.

Summer Wishes, Winter Dreams. Dir. Gilbert Cates. Wr. Stewart Stern. 1973. Videocassette. Columbia TriStar Home Video, 1987.

Sunset Boulevard. Dir. Billy Wilder. Wr. Charles Brackett, Billy Wilder, and D. M. Marshman Jr. 1950. Videocassette. Paramount Pictures, 1994.

Taxi Driver. Dir. Martin Scorsese. Wr. Paul Schrader. Columbia Pictures, 1976.

The Thin Red Line. Dir. Terrence Malick. Scr. Malik. Based on the novel by James Jones. Twentieth Century Fox, 1998.

The Three Faces of Eve. Dir. Nunnally Johnson. Scr. Johnson. 1957. Videocassette. Fox Video, 1993.

To Kill a Mockingbird. Dir. Robert Mulligan. Scr. Horton Foote. Based on the novel by Harper Lee. 1962. Videocassette. MCA Home Video, 1987.

Vertigo. Dir. Alfred Hitchcock. Scr. Alec Coppel and Samuel Taylor. Based on the novel *D'entre les morts* by Pierre Boileau and Thomas Narcejac. 1958. Restored version. Videocassette Widescreen Edition. With Limited Edition Booklet. Leland H. Faust, Patricia Hitchcock O'Connell, and Kathleen O'Connell Fiala, Trustees under the Alfred J. Hitchcock Trust, 1996.

What Ever Happened to Baby Jane? Dir. Robert Aldrich. Scr. Lukas Heller. From a novel by Henry Farrell. 1962.

A Woman under the Influence. Dir. John Cassavetes. Wr. Cassavetes. Videocassette. Touchstone Home Video, 1974.

The Wrong Man. Dir. Alfred Hitchcock. Scr. Maxwell Anderson and Angus MacPhail. 1956. Videocassette. Warner Home Video, 1999.

Index

abandonment, fear of, 48, 84

abnormality, 95, 103; inability to conform, 40–41; refusal to conform, 19

acrophobia: in *Vertigo*, 48, 59, 60, 62

Affliction, 142–43

aggressiveness, 34, 137

Agnes of God, 99–102; and ecstasy, xv

Agnes, Saint, 99–100

agoraphobia, 44

Albert, Eddie, 116

alcohol: in *Affliction*, 142–43; in *Captain Newman, M. D.*, 117; and creativity, 95; in *The Fisher King*, 104; in *The Shining*, 133; stigma of, 35; in *A Streetcar Named Desire*, 70–71; in *Taxi Driver*, 138; and violence, 134; in *A Woman under the Influence*, 13

Aldrich, Robert, 47

Alford, Philip, 5

Allen, Jay Presson, 63

All Quiet on the Western Front, 113

amnesia, 47, 48, 51, 101

Anatomy of Melancholy, 108

Anderson, Judith, 50

Andrews, Dana, 114

Andrus, Mark, 43

An Angel at My Table, 20

anger, 82; in *The Caretakers*, 35; exploitation of, 84; and injustice, 138–39; in *Marnie*, 64; and military/war, 119; in *Plenty*, 80, 81; in *Raging Bull*, 140; in *The Rain People*, 75; in *Sophie's Choice*, 86

anima, 61

anxiety, 34, 81, 116; in the general population, xvi; in *The Snake Pit*, 21, 25

Apocalypse Now, 125–30

Archer, Anne, 84

Arthurian legend, 104–5

As Good As It Gets, 43–45

Ashby, Hal, 119

asylum. *See* mental hospitals

Badham, Mary, 5

Bacon, Kevin, 81

Baker, Elliott, 93

Baker, Roy, 71

Balsam, Martin, 76
Bancroft, Anne, 73, 100
Banks, Russell: *Affliction* (novel), 142
Barrie, Barbara, 36
Barrie, James: *Peter Pan*, 77
Bartlett, Hall, 32
Beatty, Warren, 37, 107
A Beautiful Mind, xv, 92–93
Bel Geddes, Barbara, 60
Beloved, 85, 87–89
Benny & Joon, 95–96
Berenger, Tom, 121
Bergen, Polly, 33, 36
Bergman, Ingrid, 51
Bernhardt, Curtis, 82
Bernini: *The Ecstasy of Saint Theresa*, 101
Bernstein, Elmer, 33
The Best Years of Our Lives, 113–15
bipolar disease, 138; and creativity, 91
The Birds, 48, 49, 58, 59
Blake, William, 96; "The Book of Thel," 37–38
Blatty, William Peter, 106
Bogart, Humphrey, 115
"The Book of Thel," 37–38
borderline personality disorder, 49, 73–74, 84, 138
Born on the Fourth of July, 119–20
Bottoms, Sam, 128
Boyle, Peter, 138
Brando, Marlon, 70, 129
Breck, Peter, 131
Brenner, Dori, 77
Brest, Martin, 94
Bridges, Jeff, 104
Brooks, Dean R., 15
Brooks, James L., 43
Brown, Rob, 94
Burton, Richard, 102
Burton, Robert: *Anatomy of Melancholy*, 108

catatonia, 34, 51, 82, 117, 136
Caan, James, 73

The Caine Mutiny, 115–17
Campion, Jane, 20
Captain Newman, M.D., 116
The Caretakers, 32–36
Carey, Macdonald, 58
Carroll, Leo G., 51
Carter, Rosalynn: media and the movies, xiv
Cassavetes, John, xv, 11
Cates, Gilbert, 76
chaos, 107–9, 127; of major mental illnesses, xiv; and Hitchcock, 48, 58–59
Charles, Josh, 11
Chase, Ilka, 2
Chattahoochee, 119
Chechik, Jeremiah, 95
Chekhov, Michael, 52
chronic depression. *See* depression
Cimino, Michael, 122
Christ figure, 62, 142
Cleckley, Hervey M., 26
Clifford, Graeme, 20
Clift, Montgomery, 28, 30
clinical depression. *See* depression
clinics, community-based, 24, 34, 119
Close, Glenn, 84
close-up: in *The Caretakers*, 33; in *Chattahoochee*, 120; in *David and Lisa*, 41; in *Don't Bother to Knock*, 72; in *Lilith*, 109; in *Plenty*, 80; in *Repulsion*, 136; in *Sophie's Choice*, 87
Cobb, Lee J., 26
Coburn, James, 142
Coming Home, 119
Connery, Sean, 62, 93
Conrad, Joseph, 126–28; *Heart of Darkness*, 126–29
contagion: and mental illness, 25, 109
Cooke, Alistair, 26
Cooper, Gladys, 2
Coppola, Francis Ford, 73, 125
Cotton, Joseph, 56
Coyote, Peter, 111

Crane, Hart, 110
Crawford, Joan, 34, 82, 83
creativity, 2, 127; and madness, 93, 94, 107; according to Plato, 91
Crowe, Russell, 92–93
Cruise, Tom, 119

Dafoe, Willem, 121
Dali, Salvador, 52
Dance, Charles, 79
Darin, Bobby, 117
Darkness Visible: A Memoir of Madness, 17
da Silva, Howard, 39
David and Lisa, 39–41
Davis, Bette, 2
Day, Doris, 59, 107
Dead Poets Society, 8–11
DeBroca, Philippe, 130
The Deer Hunter, 122–24, 130
de Havilland, Olivia, 21
dementia praecox: See schizophrenia
De Mille, Cecil B., 70
Demme, Jonathan, 87, 133
demons: in ancient Greece, 106; in Jewish foklore, 108; and madness, 106, 107, 110–11; in the Middle Ages, 106; in the Old Testament, 106
denial of reality, 21, 25, 36; in Captain Newman, M.D., 116; in The Caretakers, 32; in Don't Bother to Knock, 72; in Equus, 102–3; in The Fisher King, 104; in Ordinary People, 41; in Sophie's Choice, 111; in A Streetcar Named Desire, 71
Deneuve, Catherine, 135
De Niro, Robert, 122, 137, 139–42
Depp, Johnny, 96
depression, 68, 82; in movies, xiv; in The Caretakers, 34, 35; in Darkness Visible: A Memoir of Madness, 17; in The Fisher King, 105; in Girl, Interrupted, 137; in Now, Voyager, 3; in Plenty, 79, 81; in The Snake

Pit, 21, 24, 25; in Sophie's Choice, 85; and war, 119
Dern, Bruce, 119
desaturated color, 86–87
DeVito, Danny, 14
Diagnostic and Statistical Manual of Mental Disorders, 81, 114
Dickens, Charles: Great Expectations, 67, 70
dissociation, 121–23
dissociative identity disorder. See multiple personality
The Divided Self, 1
Dmytryk, Edward, 28, 115
doctor-patient relationship, 2–3, 17, 18–19, 24, 26, 42–43; romanticized, 31–32, 38–39, 51
documentary, 24, 26, 72
D'Onofrio, Vincent, 124
Don't Bother to Knock, xiv–xv, 71–73, 74
The Doors: "The End," 125
Dourif, Brad, 14
Douglas, Michael, 84
Drayton, Michael, 93
dreams, 18, 61, 63, 64, 76, 114; and surrealism, 52–53, 54; versus reality, 55, 136
Dreyfuss, Richard, 18
Dullea, Keir, 39
du Maurier, Daphne: Rebecca (novel), 49
Duvall, Robert, 5, 73, 117, 127
Duvall, Shelley, 132

Eastwood, Clint, 83
echolalia, 97
"The Ecstasy of Saint Theresa," 101
ECT. See electroshock therapy
electroconvulsive therapy. See electroshock therapy
electroshock therapy, 5, 23–24, 27, 42, 97; to control or punish, 17, 34, 131; sensationalized, 35–36, 93
Eliot, T. S.: "The Hollow Men," 130

Elise, Kimberly, 87
epic, 28, 85, 87
Equus, xv, 102–3
Ermey, Lee, 124
Euripides, 131
"The Eve of St. Agnes," 100, 101
The Exorcist, 106

Falk, Peter, 11
false self: and R. D. Laing, 1; and
    pressure to conform, 2, 3–4, 13–14
Farmer, Frances, 20
Fatal Attraction, 82, 83–85
feigned madness, 131; in *Hamlet*, xiii;
    in *One Flew over the Cuckoo's Nest*,
    15
Fear Strikes Out, xv, 3–5, 36
Ferrer, Jose, 115
Finding Forrester, 94–95
A Fine Madness, 93–94
Firth, Peter, 102
The Fisher King, 124–26
flashbacks, 26, 85, 118, 142–43; in
    Beloved, 87; in *Nuts*, 18; in
    Possessed, 82; in *The Rain People*,
    75; in *Sophie's Choice*, 86–87; in
    Summer Wishes, Winter Dreams, 76
Fletcher, Louise, 14
fog filters, 61
Fonda, Jane, 100
Fonda, Peter, 108
Fontaine, Joan, 49, 50
Ford, Constance, 35
Forman, Milos, 13, 14
Forrest, Frederic, 128
Foster, Jodie, 139
Foucault, Michel: *Madness and
    Civilization*, 22; on mental hospitals,
    22
Frame, Janet, 20
Frances, 20
Francis of Assisi, 98, 99
Freud, Sigmund, 52, 54, 62, 64; and
    ego, superego, id, 28
Friedkin, William, 106

Fuller, Samuel, 131
Full Metal Jacket, 122, 124–25, 139
Furneaux, Yvonne, 135

Genn, Leo, 24
Gilliam, Terry, 104
Girl, Interrupted, 136
Glover, Danny, 88
Goldberg, Whoopi, 137
Goldman, Bo, 13
Gone with the Wind, 28
Gooding, Cuba, Jr., 44
Gothic elements, 28, 49
Great Expectations, 67, 70
Greeks: creativity and madness, 98
group therapy, 16, 34, 35, 103
Guest, Judith: *Ordinary People* (novel),
    41
guilt: in *Beloved*, 88; in *Shadow of a
    Doubt*, 58; in *Possessed*, 83; in
    Sophie's Choice; in *Spellbound*, 52,
    54; and war, 116–17

Hackman, Gene, 108
hallucinations, 34, 76, 77, 83, 101
Hamlet. See *The Tragedy of Hamlet,
    Prince of Denmark*
Hanks, Tom, 121
Hare, David: *Plenty* (play), 78
Hasford, Gustav, 124
Hauben, Lawrence, 13
Hawke, Ethan, 11
Hawthorne, Nigel, 1
Heart of Darkness, 126–29
Hedren, Tippi, 62
Heflin, Van, 82
Hemingway, Ernest, 95, 118, 119
Henreid, Paul, 3
Hepburn, Katherine, 30
Hicks, Scott, 97
Hingle, Pat, 37
Hirsch, Judd, 42
Hitchcock, Alfred, 47, 48, 63, 65, 108,
    132
Holden, William, 69

"The Hollow Men," 130
Hopkins, Anthony, 133
Hopkins, Kenyon, 107
Horace, 113
Howard, Ron, xv, 92
Hudson, Rock, 107
Hunt, Helen, 44
Hunter, Kim, 70, 109
Hush . . . Hush, Sweet Charlotte, 47
Hutton, Timothy, 41
Hyler, Steven E., 84
Hytner, Nicholas, 1

Inge, William, 36
innocence versus experience, 37–38, 39
insanity. See mental illness
insomnia, 29, 117, 138

Jackson, Mick, 120
James, William: The Varieties of Religious Experience, 98–99
Jewison, Norman, xv, 99
Johnson, Nunnally, 26
Johnson, Van, 115
Jolie, Angelina, 137
Jones, Jennifer, 117
Julius Caesar, 50
Jung, Carl, 52, 61, 127

Kantor, MacKinlay, 113
Kaysen, Susanna: Girl, Interrupted (book), 136
Kazan, Elia, 36, 70
Keats, John: "The Eve of St. Agnes," 100, 101
Kershner, Irvin, 93
Kesey, Ken: One Flew over the Cuckoo's Nest (novel), 13
King Lear, xiii
King of Hearts, 130
King, Stephen: The Shining (novel), 132
Kinnear, Greg, 43
kleptomania, 47, 48

Kline, Kevin, 85, 109
Knight, Shirley, 73
Korean War, 120
Kovic, Ron, 119
Kubrick, Stanley, 47, 122

La Motta, Jake, 139
Laing, R. D., 13; The Divided Self, 1
Lassick, Sydney, 14
Lee, Harper: To Kill a Mockingbird (novel), 5
Leigh, Vivien, 70
Le Morte Darthur, 104
Leonard, Robert Sean, 8, 11
Levine, Ted, 133
Lewis, Joe, 141
Lilith, 106
Litvak, Anatole, 21
Lloyd, Christopher, 14
Lloyd, Danny, 132
lobotomy. See psychosurgery
long shot, 14, 23, 78, 125
Losing Chase, 81–82
Lumet, Sidney, xv, 102
Lyne, Adrian, 83

MacNicol, Peter, 85, 110
madness. See mental illness
Madness and Civilization, 22
The Madness of King George, 1, 2, 11
major depression. See depression
make believe, 69, 108, 111
Malden, Karl, 3, 71
Malick, Terrence, 121
Malory, Sir Thomas: Le Morte Darthur, 104
Maltin, Leonard, 73
Mangold, James, 136
Mankiewicz, Joseph, 30
The Man in the Gray Flannel Suit, 117–19
The Man Who Knew Too Much, 48, 58, 59
March, Fredric, 113, 118
Margolin, Janet, 39

Marlowe, Christopher, 93
Marnie, 54, 58–59, 62–65; and fear of abandonment, 49; and kleptomania, 48
Massey, Raymond, 82
Masterson, Mary Stuart, 95
Mayo, Virginia, 114
melancholy, 69, 76; feeling blue, 136
memory, 70, 71, 88, 89; and amnesia, 53; benefits, 67; dangers, 77; and melancholy, 76; and nostalgia, 68, 79
mental breakdown. *See* nervous breakdown
mental collapse. *See* nervous breakdown
Mental Health: A Report of the Surgeon General, xvi
mental hospitals, 82, 97, 130; in the nineteenth century, 29; private facilities, 31, 38, 61, 136; state facilities, 4, 14, 24–25, 30, 33, 72, 120
mental illness: causes, xvi, 22, 26, 34; diagnosis/treatment of, xvi, 16–17, 19, 25, 26, 27, 28, 32, 33, 34, 38, 93, 103; difficulties in defining, 11, 12, 13–14, 15, 17, 19, 51, 55, 96; as evil, 133; and heredity, 3; image of mentally ill persons, xiv, 23; and isolation, 14, 22; legislation, 28; as mystery, xiii, xv, xvi; occurrence, xvi, 35, 56, 118; otherness, xv, 18; public's fear of, xv, 25; sensationalization of, 31, 35–36, 84, 93; stereotypes of, 5, 17, 48, 132, 134; stigma of, 8, 16, 28, 35, 36, 38, 41, 42, 92, 96, 107, 114; sympathetic portrayals, xiv–xv, 13, 22, 30, 32, 40, 45, 71–72, 82; tolerance of, 6, 8
A Midsummer Night's Dream, 10
Miles, Vera, 59
Milius, John, 126
Miller, David, 116

Mirren, Helen, 81
Monroe, Marilyn, 71, 72
Moore, Mary Tyler, 41
Moriarty, Cathy, 140
Mulligan, Robert, 3, 4, 5
Morrison, Toni: *Beloved* (novel), 87
multiple personality, 26, 27, 28, 47, 48, 65; denial of reality, 25
Munch, Edvard: *The Scream*, 33
music: and prophets, 98
mysticism, 98–99

narcissism, 108; self-absorption, 93
Nasar, Sylvia, 93
Nash, John, 92–93
Neill, Sam, 78
nervous breakdown, 2, 12, 21, 25, 36, 48, 51, 58, 76, 82, 120
nervous condition. *See* nervous breakdown
Newton, Thandie, 88
New Yorker, 61
Nicholson, Jack, 14, 43, 132
Nolte, Nick, 142–43
normality, 13, 29, 41, 88
nostalgia, 68, 76, 79, 82
Novak, Kim, 60
Now, Voyager, 2–3, 26
Nuts, 17–20, 134
Nykvist, Sven, 99

obsessions, 44, 70, 78, 107, 108, 115, 116
obsessive compulsive disorder, 44
obsessiveness, 50, 84, 89, 138
OCD. *See* obsessive compulsive disorder
"Ode: Intimations of Immortality from Recollections of Early Childhood," 36, 39
Oldman, Gary, 120
Olivier, Laurence, 49
O'Neal, Patrick, 94
One Flew over the Cuckoo's Nest, xiv–xv, 13–17

Ordinary People, 41–43, 54
Owen, Wilfred, 113, 125

Paige, Janis, 36
Pakula, Alan J., 3, 5, 85, 109
Paramount Pictures, 70
paranoia, 83, 105, 115, 140, 142; and inability to focus, 92
the past: inability to confront, 85, 86, 88, 89; managing a balance, 67–68; in *Plenty*, 79–81; preserving memory of, 67–68; in *Rebecca*, 49; recreating, 73; in *Summer Wishes, Winter Dreams*, 76–78; in *Sunset Boulevard*, 70
Peck, Gregory, 5, 51, 116, 117
perception: distortion of, 140; and mental illness, 33, 133
Perkins, Anthony, 3, 4, 48
Perry, Eleanor, 39
Perry, Frank, 39
Pesci, Joe, 140
Peter Pan, 77
Peters, Brock, 5
Phaedrus, 98
phobia, 47
Pielmeier, John, 99
Piersall, Jimmy, 3
Plato, 91; *Phaedrus*, 98
Platoon, 121
Play Misty for Me, 82, 83–84
Plenty, 78–81, 134
"Poetic Genius," 96
Polanski, Roman, 135, 136
Possessed, 82–83
Posttraumatic stress disorder, 114, 116, 138
Pounder, CCH, 95
prophets: in the Old Testament, 97, 98, 111
psyche, 47, 49, 65, 102, 127
psychiatric facilities. *See* mental hospitals
psychiatry, 52, 54, 83, 100, 102; criticism of, 18–19, 94; negative

portrayal of, xiv; sympathetic portrayal of, 24, 43
Psycho, 55, 59, 62, 121; exploitation of violence in, 132; and multiple personality, 48, 49; and stereotype, 65
psychoanalysis, 27, 50–51, 52, 62, 64, 103
psychopath, 56, 133
psychosis, 47–49, 50, 68, 69, 83
psychosurgery, 17; lobotomy, 30–31

Quinn, Aidan, 95

racism, 7, 29, 85, 87, 44
Raging Bull, 139–42
The Rain People, 73–76
Rains, Claude, 2
Raintree County, 28–30
Rapper, Irving, 2
Rawlings, Marjorie Kinnan, 111
realism, 61, 63, 71, 79, 82, 137
rear projections: and Hitchcock, 54
Rebecca, 48, 49–50, 58, 59
Redfield, William, 14
Redford, Robert, 41
Remarque, Erich Maria: *All Quiet on the Western Front*, 113
Repulsion, 135–36
Ritt, Martin, 17, 111, 134
Roberts, Stanley, 115
Robinson, Sugar Ray, 140
Romm, May E., 50
Rosen, George, 97
Rossen, Robert, 106
Rosten, Leo, 116
Rowlands, Gena, 11
Rubin, Theodore Isaac, 39
Ruehl, Mercedes, 106
Rush, Geoffrey, 97
Russell, Harold, 114
Ryder, Winona, 136

Saint, Eva Marie, 28
Salamanca, J. R.: *Lilith* (novel), 106

Sampson, Will, 14
Sargent, Alvin, 41
Savage, John, 121, 122
Saving Private Ryan, 121
The Scent of a Woman, 94–95
Schepisi, Fred, 78, 134
schizophrenia, 30, 39, 83, 85, 97, 107; symptoms of, 34, 95; versus stereotype, 109; and voices, 92
Schneider, Irving, 43
Schrader, Paul, 139, 142
Schulman, Tom, 8
scorned woman, 82, 83
Scorsese, Martin, 137, 139
The Scream, 33
Seberg, Jean, 94, 107
self: divided, 1, 3; false, 5, 13, 20; shadow, 125, 127; and pressure to conform, 2, 4, 5, 8, 12, 13–14, 20; public versus private, 1, 2, 11; unconscious, 122, 127; unrealized, 61
self-image, 73, 137
self-mutilation, 137
Selznick, David O., 50
sexuality, 37, 135, 138; repressed female, 76; repressed male, 137
Shadow of a Doubt, 48, 56–58, 59, 61
Shaffer, Peter: *Equus* (play), 102
Shakespeare, William: character of madman in plays, xiii–xiv, 105; *Hamlet*, xiii–xv, xvi–xvii; *Julius Caesar*, 50; *A Midsummer Night's Dream*, 10
Sheen, Charlie, 121
Sheen, Martin, 125
shell shock. *See* posttraumatic stress disorder
Shepherd, Cybill, 138
Sherwood, Robert, 113
Shine, 97
The Shining, 47, 132
Shock Corridor, 131
shock treatment. *See* electroshock therapy

Sidney, Sylvia, 76
The Silence of the Lambs, 133
slow-motion photography, 141–42
Smith, Kurtwood, 9
The Snake Pit, 21–25, 32, 33, 40, 54; and realism, 26, 28, 36; sympathetic portrayal of mental illness, xiv–xv
Socrates, 98
Sophie's Choice, 85–87, 109
Spacek, Sissy, 142
Spellbound, 48, 49, 50–55, 58, 61, 62
Splendor in the Grass, 36–39
Spoto, Donald, 49
Stack, Robert, 34, 36
Steenburgen, Mary, 111
Stevens, Mark, 22
Stewart, James, 59, 60, 107
stigmata, 98, 99, 101
Sting, 80
Stone, Oliver, 119, 121
Streep, Meryl, 78, 85, 109
A Streetcar Named Desire, 70–71, 74
Streisand, Barbra, 17
stress, xvi, 64, 120, 121
Styron, William: *Darkness Visible: A Memoir of Madness*, 17; *Sophie's Choice* (novel) 85, 109
subconscious, 52
Suddenly, Last Summer, 28–32
suicide, 29, 41, 51, 62, 69, 84, 86, 111, 123, 137
Summer Wishes, Winter Dreams, 76–78, 82
Sunset Boulevard, 67, 68–70, 74
the supernatural, 87, 89, 91, 97, 98, 110
surrealism, 52–53, 54
Sutherland, Donald, 41
Swanson, Gloria, 68
Sybil, 27

Taxi Driver, 137–39
Taylor, Elizabeth, 28, 30
Tennyson, Alfred, Lord: "Ulysses," 9
Theresa of Avila, 98, 99
Thigpen, Corbett H., 26

The Thin Red Line, 121
Thoreau, Henry David, 9; *Walden*, 8
The Three Faces of Eve, 25–28, 32, 39
Tilley, Meg, 99
To Kill a Mockingbird, 5–8, 33
tongues: and prophets, 97
Torrey, E. Fuller, 134, 134–35
The Tragedy of Hamlet, Prince of Denmark, xiii, xiv, xv, xvi–xvii, 15, 129

Ullman, Tracey, 79

The Varieties of Religious Experience, 98
vertigo, 48, 60, 61, 62
Vertigo, 48, 49, 59–62, 107
Vidal, Gore, 30
Vietnam War, 119, 121, 122, 123, 125; Tet offensive, 124
violence, 94, 116; and demons, 106; exploitation of 132, 133; film treatment of, 72–73, 135, 139, 140, 142, 143; link to mental illness, 134; management of violent patients, 34; of mentally ill to others, 80; of mentally ill to selves, 136–37; random, 121; and scorned women, 69, 82, 83, 84; and stereotype of the maniac, 109
voice-over narration, 7, 22, 120, 125
voices, 22, 34, 92, 93, 96, 99, 101, 104
Voight, Jon, 119
Van Sant, Gus, 95
von Stroheim, Erich, 68

Wahl, Otto F., xiv, 133, 134
Walden, 8

Walken, Christopher, 122
Wallach, Eli, 18
Walter, Jessica, 84, 107
Ward, Mary Jane: *The Snake Pit* (book), 21
Wayne, David, 26
Weir, Peter, 8
West Side Story, 33
What Ever Happened to Baby Jane?, 47
Whitman, Walt, 3, 110
Widmark, Richard, 72
Wilder, Billy, 68, 70
Williams, Robin, 8, 104
Williams, Tennessee, 31; *A Streetcar Named Desire* (play), 70; *Suddenly, Last Summer* (play), 30
Wilson, Sloan, 117
Winfrey, Oprah, 87
Wolfe, Thomas, 110
woman's film, 82
A Woman under the Influence, xv, 11–13
Wood, Natalie, 37
Woodward, Joanne, 26, 76, 94
Wordsworth, William, 37; "Ode: Intimations of Immortality from Recollections of Early Childhood," 36, 39
World War I, 113, 130
World War II, 70, 77, 78, 94, 107, 113, 115, 116, 117, 119, 121
Wouk, Herman: *The Caine Mutiny* (novel), 115
Wright, Teresa, 56, 114
The Wrong Man, 48, 58, 59
Wyler, William, 113

~

About the Author

Jacqueline Noll Zimmerman has worked as a writer, technical editor, and communications manager at several health care organizations, including Spectrum Emergency Care/ARA Services and the American Red Cross. She was a technical editor and instructor of writing at McDonnell Douglas Corporation (now Boeing Aircraft).

Dr. Zimmerman has a Ph.D. in English language and literature from the University of Maryland in College Park and has taught film, writing, and literature courses at the University of Maryland, Southern Illinois University in Edwardsville, Bowling Green State University, Maryville University in St. Louis, Missouri, and Lewis and Clark Community College in Godfrey, Illinois. She earned her B.A. and M.A. degrees at Southern Illinois University, Edwardsville.

Dr. Zimmerman resides in Carlinville, Illinois, with her husband, Roger, and her Schipperke, SamToo. She is currently writing a book of essays about depression.